LONG TIME, OLDEN TIME

Aboriginal accounts of Northern Territory history

collected and edited by
Peter and Jay Read

Institute for Aboriginal Development Publications

National Library of Australia
Cataloguing-in-Publication entry:
Long Time, Olden Time.
    ISBN 0 949659 58 4
    ISBN 0 949659 59 2 (set).
    [1]. Aborigines, Australian — Northern Territory — History — Sources. 2. Northern
    Territory — History — Sources. 3. Northern Territory — Race relations — Sources. I. Read,
    Peter, 1945–   . II. Read, Jay. III. Institute for Aboriginal Development (Alice Springs, N.T.).
994.29

© 1991 Peter and Jay Read

Published by the Institute for Aboriginal Development, 3 South Terrace, Alice Springs, N. T.
Designed by Christine Bruderlin, IAD Design Services. Maps by Brenda Thornley, IAD Design
Services. Unless otherwise credited, photographs are by Peter and Jay Read. Cover design
and illustration by Christine Bruderlin.
Printed by Robert Burton Printers, Sydney.

Tape 1 Side 1
Start of tape

Long time, olden time, no white people bin here. Nothing.

Nothing.

Only Napperby [*Station*], that way, and Hermannsburg. That's all. Two. Alice Spring. Two.

My father travel from here, he bin travel north, right up Hermannsburg. Him bin gettem blanket, clothes, bush knife, and axe, there. Him bin go back:

'Ah, I think I gotta go back, same place, country.'

You know, olden people, long time ago, they bin walking round everyway. Everyway. Not jealous business. . . not jealous business, not like white people, you know that, not allowed comin' through fence, 'nother place, you know white people.

No jealous for country.

No, olden people they bin walking round, now go back longa 'nother place.

Freer. Its freer. You know why? No fence, no jealous business for country. No.

Freer.

Dinny Japaljarri, Warlpiri, Yuendumu
9 August 1977

Contents

	Preface	vi
	Acknowledgements	vii
	The language of the stories	viii
	Chronology of events	ix
	List of speakers with language/tribal affiliation	xiii
	Glossary	xiv
	Map of the Northern Territory	xv
	Part One: Conflict	1
	Chapter One: The organisation of forces	
Tape 1 Side 1	A first encounter: Alec Jupurrula Wilson [not on tape]	3
	The work of a black tracker: Hickey Hood Janbuyin	4
	A black policeman in action: Fred Booth Minmienadji	5
	A first encounter with gunfire: Daly Pulkara	7
	Keeping watch: Gertie Huddleston Kurrakain	8
	The death of a police tracker: Hickey Hood Janbuyin	9
	A hill-top ambush: Hoppy Tommy Wanindyulgari	10
	A massacre at Hodgson Downs: Chicken Gonagun and Sandy Mambookyi	12
	Revenge at Elcho Island: Stephen Bunbaijan	16
	A massacre at Mirki: Anon [not on tape]	19
	A baby's life saved at the Elsey: Jess Roberts Garalnganjag and Maudie Manguj	24
	An execution in the Roper Valley: Gertie Huddleston Kurrakain	25
	Attack and counter attack at Bowgan Station: Jack Cotton Mobalily	26
	The death of Brigalow Bill: Daly Pulkara	29
	An eye-witness account of the same event [not on tape]	31
	Chapter Two: A homeland deserted: the Coniston Massacre, 1928	
	Summary of events [not on tape]	33
Tape 1 Side 2	The death of Fred Brooks: Blind Alec Jupurrula and Engineer Jack Japaljarri	35
	The discovery of Brooks' body and the formation of the first police party: Tim Japangardi	37
	Murder at Mission Creek: Jimmy Jungarrayi	39
	A second White man attacked: the assault on Nugget Morton: Willowra Jimmy Jungarrayi and Jampijinpa	40
	The massacre at Tipinpa: Jampijinpa	44
	The police party shifts to the Hanson River: Willowra Jimmy Jungarrayi	46
	A warning: Sandy Jungarrayi	47
	The massacre at Wajinpulungk: Johnny Nelson Jupurrula	48
	Months later: discovering the bodies: Charlie Jakamarra	52
	Years later: a homeland deserted: Dinny Japaljarri	52
	Like bullock: Jimmy Jungarrayi	54
	Chapter Three: Victoria River Downs, 1895–6	55
	The attack on Mulligan and Ligar: Big Mick Kankinang	56
	The massacre at Gordon Creek: Little Mick Yinyuwinma	57
	Extracts from the Gordon Creek Police Journal [not on tape]	61
	Chapter Four: Milingimbi, 1927	
Tape 2 Side 1	Missionaries attacked at Milingimbi: Willi Walilepa	63
	Another eye-witness account: Mick Makani	68

	Epilogue: The people come quiet now: Maudie Manguj and Jess Roberts Garalnganjag	68
	Part Two : Living with Whites	71
	Chapter One: Coming in	73
	Making a choice at the Elsey: Jess Roberts Garalnganjag	74
	He got half our boy belong to us now: Powder O'Keefe	76
	I want the boys for the school: Clancy Warrawilya	78
	All right, you can stop for couple of days: Riley Young Winpilin	80
	Plenty short tucker: Jampijinpa	83
	The old people or the new: Tim Janama	84
	In search of tobacco: Engineer Jack Japaljarri	87
Tape 2 Side 2	Exchange at Groote Eylandt: Ninawunda Jerakba	90
	Because with his son he must come back: Johnny Nelson Jupurrula	91
	Keep away from waterhole: Sandy Jungarrayi	92
	Extract from the Barrow Creek Police Station Journal [not on tape]	93
	Chapter Two: Learning the alien culture	94
	Baking powder: Jerry Jangala	94
	Flour, tobacco and matches: Rory Wudul Biyangunu	95
	The dormitory: Topsy Nelson Napurrula	97
	Language: Hagar Roberts	101
	The Big House: Leslie Wunuwugu	104
	Chapter Three: Living and working	
	Do you want a job?: George Huddleston	105
	Teaching the pastoralist: Big Mick Kankinang	107
	Tin mining: Spider Brennan	109
Tape 3 Side 1	Droving: Kaiser Bill Jaluba	114
	Chapter Four: The Second World War	122
	Recruitment — north: Sandy August Liwiliwirri	122
	Recruitment — south: Jampijinpa	123
	Training: Tim Japangardi	125
	A friendly sergeant: Stephen Bunbaijan	126
	Sundays: Stephen Watson Narweya	128
	Pay day: Tracker Tommy	128
	An air-raid at Darwin: Tim Japangardi	129
	An air-raid at Milingimbi: Eva Number One	130
	Taking prisoners: Jimmy Jungarrayi	132
	Good times: Tim Japangardi	133
	Good times: Jampijinpa	133
	A European account of life at the Alice Springs Aboriginal camp: Johnno O'Keefe [not on tape]	134
	Chapter Five: After the War	136
	A police tracker: Tracker Tommy	136
Tape 3 Side 2	You're not allowed to marry whitefeller: Alma Gibb	141
	Two views on traditional law:	
	(a) You can't change the law: Nelli Camfoo Papi	144
	(b) This thing should be tellem the young fellers. But nothing: Jack Cotton Mobalily	145
	Mainoru to Bulman: Willi Martin Jaylama	146
	Elsey to Djembere (Jilkminggan): Jess Roberts Garalnganjag	148
	Epilogue: following the direction: Worraki Number One	150

Preface

This book is composed of interviews with Aboriginal people of the Northern Territory recorded in 1976–7. The recordings were commissioned by the Northern Territory Department of Education and were intended to be used as a school text. The Department, however, declined to make use of the material, which remained unheard and unread for more than a decade. In 1989 the Institute for Aboriginal Development, Alice Springs, suggested that the recordings be published, partly for use as course material for adult education courses, and partly for a wider Australian audience.

Our first thought, as editors, was that the recordings would need to be brought up to date to take account of the changes since the interviews took place. When we listened to them, however, we realised that the fifteen years which had elapsed since the recordings had encapsulated the memories, reflections and stories into the particular view of the mid 1970s. Since then, much has changed. In the mid 1970s Homeland Centres, still known as outstations, were still few and experimental. Eye-witnesses to the Coniston massacre were still living, as were men and women who could recall the time when certain areas were still totally unpenetrated by Whites. By 1990 very many of the older speakers in this book had died and most of their stories with them. Therefore we decided to leave the manuscript much as it had been prepared for publication in 1978, as the voice of a generation which has passed, or is now passing, away.

It is now more common for oral historians to reproduce interviews with a number of people as full personal statements rather than extracting segments illustrating certain aspects of Australian history chosen by editors or interviewers. Perhaps, if we were editing the interviews again we too would follow individuals rather than topics. To undertake that task now would be to alter the book as conceived in 1975 beyond recognition. So the arrangement of the book remains as it was, and to this extent reflects our own preoccupations of the late 1970s, which are now as frozen in time as the perceptions of the speakers.

It is also common, in reproducing oral texts, to leave out questions, and make whatever adjustments are necessary to make the omissions unnoticeable. But when the original recording is provided along with the transcription, as is the case in this book, very little licence is possible. Where, for clarity, we have edited the responses to questions, the break in the 'atmosphere' is usually apparent. Apart from that, we have resisted the temptation to edit the questions, and those who may find them sometimes silly or misleading may reflect that interviewers' questions often sound like this, but in radio programs, or in books where the original tapes are not reproduced, they are generally edited or omitted altogether.

The setting out of the text may look odd at first sight. The reason is that oral language is a different method of communication to written language, and since this book is meant to be heard as well as read, we have followed the flow of the spoken words in preference to the conventions of standard written English. We hope the advantages of this will become apparent once the tapes are heard.

Peter and Jay Read

Acknowledgements

The project was made possible through the generous help of the following settlements, stations and towns:
Alice Springs, Barunga, Beswick, Borroloola, Brunette Downs, Bulman, Daly River, Jilkminggan, Elliott, Galiwin'ku, Hodgson Downs, Katherine, Lajamanu, Milingimbi, Mountain Valley, Ngukurr, Nutwood Downs, Pine Creek, Umbakumba, Alekarenge (Ali Curung), Willowra, Yarralin, Yuendumu.

The editors wish particularly to thank individuals who made introductions or helped in the day to day management: Ranald Allen, Diane Bell, Con and Trish Boekel, Tex and Nellie Camfoo, Allan Christopher, Gill Cowlishaw, Ted and Chris Furbey, John and Kerry Haines, Warren Hastings, Gertie Huddleston, Jess Roberts Garalnganjag, Julie Janson, Jimmy Jungarrayi, Dick Kimber, Dick Kurnock, Ludo Kuipers, Tom Lackner, David McClay, Ivan Mamarika, Jampijinpa, Margot Reynolds, Barbara Tynan, Jim Wafer, Petronella Wafer, Marie Yeardley.

We are grateful to the following for their professional assistance and advice: Jim Cameron, Tamsin Donaldson, Michael Christie, Judy Cox, Russell Goldflam, Ian Green, Stephen Harris, Dick Kimber, Francesca Merlan, Paddy Naughton, Karen Smith, Jim Urry, Ian Whelan.

We acknowledge the generous assistance of the Australian Institute of Aboriginal and Torres Strait Islander Studies and the Institute for Aboriginal Development.

Permission to reproduce the text
Those who first consented to be recorded gave their permission to use the material in the book as it was originally conceived. One or two people whose stories were recorded by other interviewers also gave their permission. Since such a long time has elapsed, the authors have wherever possible contacted the speakers to ask that permission to reproduce these tapes be renewed. This was granted in almost every case.

In the years since the recordings, many of the speakers have died, and in these cases the authors have renegotiated permission with relatives of the speakers. We thank both the speakers and their relatives for allowing us to use the stories so long after they were first recorded.

In several cases it has not been possible, despite many endeavours, to locate certain of the speakers, particularly in areas where former community living areas have ceased to exist.

The language of the stories

There are many thousands of people in the Northern Territory who use a language other than English as their first language, from the Pitjantjatjara and Warlpiri in the south and west to Burarra and Alyawarre in the north and east. The stories in *Long Time, Olden Time*, however, have been recorded by speakers using varieties of standard English known as Aboriginal English and Kriol. These varieties of English have developed over many years from a number of sources to become, for many people, a first language in themselves, and contain some features of grammar that may appear unusual to the reader unfamiliar with them.

One feature of particular interest to readers of this book is the common Aboriginal English verb-ending often spelled '-em' or '-im', for example in,

'They bin cuttem wood there now"

Whilst this ending clearly derives from a casual pronunciation of the standard English words '(h)im' and '(th)em', the meaning of this ending is different from these standard words and does not necessarily refer to a particular thing or things as 'him' or 'them' does. The ending indicates that the verb, in this case 'cut', is one where the doer of the action focusses on, or affects, someone or something; in this example, the wood. The ending is not found on verbs like 'go' or 'sleep' where the doer of the action does not focus on or directly affect anything.

Another point to note is that most traditional Aboriginal languages do not distinguish between masculine and feminine pronouns ('he' and 'she'), having only one word which can be used to refer to either a male or a female. In the following example, the reader might well be confused about who the 'him' is;

'And so the old man let her go, that old lady. That Freddie took him away, washing clothes…',

although the wider context would suggest that it is the woman.

As well as these instances of differing grammatical features, the reader will encounter words that either differ in meaning from standard English, or have been brought into Aboriginal English from further afield. Many Europeans, apparently in ignorance of the diversity of Aboriginal languages, brought with them words from other Aboriginal languages which had become part of the pidgin used between Aboriginal people and English speakers in other places. Central Australian 'myall', for example, meaning roughly 'uncivilised', came originally from the Dharuk language of the Sydney area. Some words from traditional Aboriginal languages have been retained in Aboriginal English, while in other cases a standard English word is used with the meaning of a traditional language word. 'Cheeky' is used in Alice Springs Aboriginal English with the meaning of words like 'ahe-akngerre' in Arrernte or 'pikati' in Pitjantjatjara, something like 'aggressive, angry', which is subtly different from the standard English meaning.

The above examples show how a reader may misinterpret a sentence or story, a problem that can be compounded in a text-only oral history where the additional meaning lent by the intonation of the speaker's voice is lost. Previous attempts to clarify written Aboriginal English stories by altering them to standard English have often lead to the criticism that they are no longer transcriptions but translations, and that the text no longer represents a wholly Aboriginal view. Thus, the importance of reproducing the original stories on a series of audio cassettes becomes obvious, presenting the stories to the reader/listener with the minimum of editorial interference.

Words and phrases used commonly in Aboriginal English that appear throughout the text have been included in a glossary at the front of the book and these, with the map and linking historical text, provide a meaningful context in which to read and listen to the stories.

Chronology of events in Northern Territory history since 1820

	Events in NT History	Establishment of pastoral stations, settlements, missions	Changes in legislation relating to Aboriginals	Events recorded in this book
1820	Fort Dundas (Apsley St,1824) Fort Wellington (Raffles Bay, 1827)			Throughout the century, the Macassans visit the north Australian coast to gather trepang
1830	Port Essington (Victoria, 1838)			
1840	Leichhardt reaches Port Essington via the 'Gulf Route' from Qld (1844)			
1850	Gregory travels from the Victoria River to the Gulf (1856)			
1860	McDouall Stuart crosses Australia south to north (1862) NT separated from NSW, administered by SA (1863)			
1870	Darwin established (1870) Overland Telegraph Line completed (1872) Chinese brought from Singapore to work Pine Creek gold mines (l875) Stocking of central Australian stations by north–south route (1870s) Favenc discovers 'Barkly Route' from Queensland to NT (1879)	Undoolya, Owen Springs (first central Australian pastoral stations) Hermannsburg (1877) Glencoe (first northern cattle station) (1879)	Sub-protectors of Aboriginals appointed (l877)	Barrow Creek Massacre (1874)

ix

1880	One fifth of NT taken up in pastoral leases (1882) Stocking of NT via the 'Barkly Route' (1880s) Murranji Track (1886) Railway: Darwin–Pine Creek completed (1889)	Alexandria Downs, Elsey (1882) Brunette Downs, Victoria River Downs (1883) Hodgson Downs (1884) Florida (1885)	Willshire's 'native police' established in centre (1884)	Daly River Massacre (1884) Queensland drover ambushed (1880s) *1/1 First encounter with guns on the Victoria River (c.1886) *1/3 Bush people come to Alexandria (1880s) Hickey Hood's father recruited as police tracker (c.1886) *1/1 Chinese and Daly River tribes begin living together (1880s)
1890	NT cattle under quarantine because of red-water fever; slump in the industry (1897)	Gordon Downs (1895)	As yet no attempt to regulate conditions of labour.	Mangarayi and Yangman people settle at Elsey Station (1890s) *2/1 Mulligan and Ligar speared in Jasper Gorge; massacre at Gordon Creek (1895) *1/3 Attack on Macassans and resulting massacre of Elcho Islanders (c.1898) *1/1
1900	A higher population of Chinese than Europeans in Darwin, (1900s) Macassans prevented from trepanging (1907)	Roper River Mission (1908)		Murder of Brigalow Bill (1909) *1/1
1910	Commonwealth Govt. assumes NT administration (1911)	Bathurst Island Mission (1910) Goulburn Island Mission (1916)	NT Aborigines Act: a Chief Protector appointed and an Aborigines Department. Chief Protector has wide powers over Aboriginals and part-Aboriginals (1911)	Hagar Roberts learns a European culture (c.1916) *2/2 Fred Booth in charge of a droving team joins a punitive expedition. (c.1916) *1/1

* Numbers refer to the part and chapter in which reference is made

1910	Outbreak of World War I (1914); many White men enlist, Aboriginals given jobs of greater responsibility in the absence of White labour.		Royal Commission states that the number of 'full-blood' Aboriginals was decreasing (1913) Ordinance of the NT regulates employment of Aboriginals in towns, allows missions to care for children (1918)	Massacre at Bowgan Station (c.1919) *1/1 Massacre at Hodgson Downs (c.1917) *1/1 Tim Janama joins Captain Luff (c.1910 – 20) *2/1
1920	Drought in central Australia (1924–8) Railway: Oodnadatta–Alice Springs completed (1927)	Oenpelli Aboriginal Reserve (1920) Emerald River Mission (Groote Eylandt) (1921) Daly River Reserve (1923) Oenpelli Mission (1925)	Bleakley Report recommends payment of minimum wages to Aboriginals (1928) Aboriginals Ordinance decrees that only the Chief Protector could issue licences to employ Aboriginals (1928)	Ninawunda Jerakba trades shell for tobacco at Emerald River (1920s) *2/1 Robertson speared at Milingimbi (1927) *1/4 M.C. Murray chases bush people away from settled areas (1928) *1/2 Engineer Jack and the Warrmarla visit Wave Hill (1928) *2/1 Coniston Massacre (1928) *1/2
1930	Granites Gold rush (1932) Wolfram gold discovered at Tennant Creek (1933) Wolfram mining in Coniston area (early 1930s) Constable McColl speared at Woodah Island (1933) Outbreak of World War II (1939)	Haasts Bluff Reserve (1930) Arnhem Land Reserve (1931) Port Keats Mission (1935) Jay Creek (1937)	Aboriginals Ordinance: wages set for drovers and some Aboriginals (1933) Commonwealth-State Conference: first phase of the government policy swing from 'protection' to 'assimilation' (1937)	Spider Brennan recruited at Maranboy (c.1930) *2/3 Kaiser Bill learns droving at Montejinnie (c.1930) *2/3 Tracker Tommy recruited as a police tracker (c.1933) *2/5 Big Mick Kankinang shows country to VRD Manager (c.1935) *2/3 Clancy Warrawilya brought to Umbakumba (c.1938) *2/1

* Numbers refer to the part and chapter in which reference is made

1940	First air raid on Darwin (1942)	Areyonga (1943)	Conditions of employment and rate of pay laid down by Dept of Army (1945)	Air raids on Milingimbi (1942) *2/4
		Phillip Creek (1946)		Leslie Wunuwugu grows up (1940s) at Urapunga *2/2
		Yuendumu (1946)	Carrington reports pastoral wages mostly in kind (1945)	
		Beswick (1949)		Topsy Nelson runs away from the Phillip Creek mission (1949) *2/2
		Lajamanu (Hooker Creek) (1949)		
			Pastoral wages set at £2 p.w. for experienced men (1947)	
1950		Warrabri (Alekarenge) (1955)	Wards Employment Ordinance (1953)	N.A.B. tries to prevent cohabitation at Beswick (c.1950)
		Papunya (1956)		
		Pintubi Reserve (1959)		
1960	Gurindji walk-off at Wave Hill (1966)	Amoonguna (1960)	Voting rights given to Aboriginals (1962)	Some station people leave Elsey, Mainoru, Victoria Downs for independent settlements
	General relaxing of White control at mission stations (late 1960s)		Repeal of Wards Ordinance (1964)	
			Aboriginal stockmen granted pay equal to White stockmen (1966)	
			Commonwealth Government given concurrent power to legislate for Aboriginals by Referendum (1967)	
1970	'Homeland' or 'Outstation' movement gathers strength		Gove Land Rights case (1971)	
			Establishment of N.A.C.C. (1972)	
	NT receives self-government (1978)		Aboriginal Land Rights Commission Report (1974)	
			Aboriginal Land Rights (NT) Act (1976)	

* Numbers refer to the part and chapter in which reference is made

Speakers
with language/tribal affiliation and location of interview

Spider Brennan, Ngalakan, Barunga and Maranboy
Daly Pulkara, Ngarinman, Yarralin
Stephen Bunbaijan Liyagalawumirr, Galiwin'ku
Anon, Milingimbi
Eva Number One, Milingimbi
Jess Roberts Garalnganjag, Mangarayi, Jilkminggan
Chicken Gonagun, Alawa, Hodgson Downs
George Huddleston, Mudburra, Pine Creek
Little Mick Yinyuwinma, Ngaliwuru, Yarralin and Police Hole
Charlie Jakamarra, Warlpiri, Willowra
Kaiser Bill Jaluba, Mudburra, Katherine and Murranji Track
Jampijinpa, Warlpiri, Willowra, Boomerang Hole and Tipinpa
Tim Janama, Yanuywa, Borroloola
Hickey Hood Janbuyin, Mangarayi, Barunga
Dinny Japaljarri, Warlpiri, Yuendumu
Engineer Jack Japaljarri, Warlpiri, Alekarenge
Tim Japangardi, Warlpiri, Yuendumu
Willy Martin Jaylama, Rembarrnga, Bulman
Ninawunda Jerakba, Wanindilyakwa, Umbakumba
Jimmy Jungarrayi, Warlpiri, Willowra
Jimmy Jungarrayi, Warlpiri, Yuendumu
Sandy Jungarrayi, Warlpiri, Willowra
Blind Alec Jupurrula, Warlpiri, Alekarenge
Johnny Nelson Jupurrula, Warlpiri, Alekarenge
Alec Wilson Jupurrula, Warlpiri, Mount Doreen Station
Big Mick Kankinang, Ngaliwuru, Yarralin and Jasper Gorge
Gertie Huddleston Kurrakain, Warndarang, Ngukurr
Sandy August Liwiliwirri, Alawa, Hodgson Downs Station
Sandy Mambookyi, Alawa, Hodgson Downs Station
Fred Booth Minmienadji, Kurdanji, Brunette Downs Station
Jack Cotton Mobalily, Wambaya, Brunette Downs
Maudie Munguj, Mangarayi, Jilkminggan
Topsy Nelson Napurrula, Kaytej, Alekarenge and Phillip Creek
Stephen Watson Narweya, Maung, Katherine
Nelli Camfoo Papi, Rembarrnga, Bulman
Powder O'Keefe, Kurdanji Brunette Downs
Hagar Roberts, Alawa, Nutwood Downs Station
Tracker Tommy, Jingili, Elliott
Willi Walilepa, Galiwin'ku
Hoppy Tommy Wanindyulgari, Alawa, Nutwood Downs Station
Clancy Warrawilya, Wanindilyakwa, Umbakumba
Riley Young Winpilin, Ngarinman, Yarralin
Worraki Number One (translated by Bilu, Djambarrpuyngu), Dharlwangu, Galiwin'ku
Leslie Wunuwugu, Alawa, Hodgson Down Station
Rory Wudul Biyangunu, Garrwa, Borroloola
Mick Makani, Djinang, Galiwin'ku
Jerry Jangala, Warlpiri, Lajamanu
Alma Gibb, Rembarrnga

Glossary

Aborigin	Aboriginal pronunciation of 'Aborigine'
Balanda	White person
boy	Aboriginal man
bush tucker	food obtained from the bush, for instance, kangaroo, berries
business	Aboriginal religious ceremonial activity
cheeky	aggressive, disrespectful, dangerous, bad
coolamon	wooden or bark carrying trough
country	as in 'my country': land that has particular spiritual relationship to an Aboriginal person
countryman	person from the same tribal area or group
European	white person
finished	ended, died, destroyed
grow (me) up	care for (me) as a child until grown up
he/his/him	(where appropriate) she/hers/her
kill	(generally) hit, injure
law	custom and tradition dictating Aboriginal sacred and secular behaviour
Macassans	Indonesian fishermen who visited the north coast of Australia to gather trepang (beche de mer)
myall	Aboriginal person who has not had much contact with Europeans. Often used derogatively
nikki-nikki	low-grade black twist tobacco which formerly made up part of Aboriginal rations
outstation	originally a secondary establishment on a cattle station, now often used to mean independent Aboriginal camps away from main settlements
perish	die (of exposure)
promise system	system of arranged marriages: a woman arranged to marry a certain man is known as his 'promise'
proper	genuine, real
quieten	to make bush people more tractable, peaceable, often having sinister overtones because of the violence involved.
rubbish	no good, outdated, broken, valueless
subsection, 'skin'	system of dividing a tribal group into a number of sections. Used as a means of defining a person's relationship with others.
sugarbag	wild bush honey
(he) talk language	(he) spoke in an Aboriginal language.
yuwayi, yu	yes
Yolngu	Aboriginal people (East Arnhem Land)SS

The Northern Territory

Part One

Conflict

Chapter One
The organisation of forces

'We have fought no battles for our soil, no revolution, no glorious struggles for liberation and. . . no agonies of a turbulent history.'
The Sunday Australian, 25 April 1971

Not recorded on accompanying tape

A first encounter

Alec Jupurrula Wilson, Warlpiri, Mount Doreen Station

Alec Jupurrula Wilson

The European exploration of the Northern Territory took over seventy years to complete. The meeting described below occurred in the 1920s, almost at the end of the period. Alec Jupurrula Wilson travelled the region west of the Granites with white men acting as interpreter between them and the Warlpiri.

Another lot of Whites turned up . . . with camels this time. Two unarmed Warlpiri men went up to them and made friends with them. The Whites with the camels asked them where to find water. The men took the Whites to a waterhole where they met up with another group of Warlpiri people camped there. These people then picked out two more guides for the Whites whom they led to the next waterhole where yet another pair of guides was found. The original guides would then return to their group . . .

About 1928 when these people *[Whites]* came through here with me as their guide and interpreter they came across one of the last lot of people who had never seen a white man. They were wild but they didn't hinder the Whites. They would just show them the waterholes and let them go through their country. The Warlpiri used to hunt for meat — kangaroo, rabbits and wild-cats. That was their only meat.

The Whites didn't interfere with the Warlpiri women at that time because the women used to run away frightened and hide in the bush along with some of the very old people about eighty.

As for some of the middle-aged men, when they saw the Whites approaching,

Members of the Horne & Aiston Expedition to the Northern Territory (G. Horne & G. Aiston, Savage Life in Central Australia, London, MacMillan & Co., 1924)

they would wait for them and go to meet them.

In those days the wild bush Aboriginals didn't fight with the Whites. It was only the ones who were a 'bit civilized' who used to fight with the Whites.

The years 1870–1910 enclose the period when the pastoralists from South Australia and Queensland came in sufficient numbers to challenge the Aboriginal ascendancy over the better pastoral areas. Besides the Chinese and other gold-diggers, speculators and adventurers, there may have been eight or nine large droving and settlement parties passing through Anthony Lagoon or Alice Springs in any one year. Unlike the White men in the above account, the new arrivals intended to stay and many were prepared to use any methods to drive the Aborigines from the land.

To retain the land was no easier task than subduing it. Tempe Downs, Florida, Willeroo and Delamere Stations were among many which were abandoned temporarily or permanently due in part to continuing Aboriginal hostility. Throughout this period Whites locked their doors and slept with a revolver under the pillow. When travelling, it was common to unroll the swag inside a mosquito net, then sleep in a tree.

Tape 1 Side 1

The work of a black tracker

Hickey Hood Janbuyin, Mangarayi, Barunga

Hickey Hood Janbuyin describes how his father was spared, during a White 'punitive raid' against the bush people in the Kimberleys, because he 'knew the country' and would act as an unofficial 'native policeman'. The sparing of such children for tracking or domestic service seems to have been a common occurrence. This event probably took place in the 1890s.

*Hickey Hood
Janbuyin*

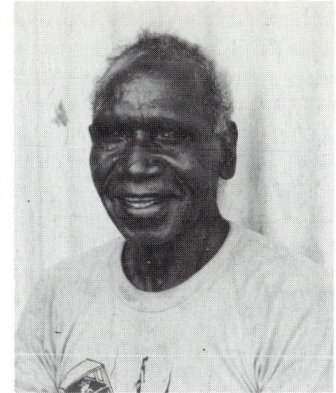

My old father bin doin' like that. My father bin go shooting you know. All over here. Start up from Kimberley.

Right round, all round that Alice Spring. Come round this way, all over 'nother lot. They all split, you know, split up. Half go this way, half comin' this way. My father bin longa this lot, he blongta Kimberley, my father too.

He come on from there, comin' down this way.

Shootin' all round there.

Who were they shooting?

Shootem blackfeller.
All wild blackfeller you know. That bin name, blackfeller, before. He got a new name, Aborigine.

Why did they shoot them, do you know?

Well, White man no wantem my colour, like, blackfeller. Want to try shootem whole lot, finishem up, finish all blackfeller. They want to take over this place.
My father bin longa that lot too. He bin wild one. Policeman caughtem him, you know, grabbem, holdem up:

'No more shootem that man. We'll takem. We'll keepem. We wantem. He know all the country. We want to go, look round.'

They wanted to use him as a kind of policeman, black policeman?

He want to work under policeman now, you know. Go round all round. Show all the country, all the place got blackfeller big mob, blackfeller.

Used to go there, you know, all round,

'Where that 'nother mob. You know 'nother mob?'

They talk longa language. My father bin proper really myall [bushman].

Tape 1 Side 1

A black policeman in action

Fred Booth Minmienadji, Kurdanji, Brunette Downs

The details of this story are not clear. The event seems to have taken place south of Tennant Creek in about 1917. Perhaps in the absence of White stockmen, enlisted in the armed services, Fred Booth Minmienadji may have joined a droving party and become involved in a 'punitive expedition'.

The organisation of forces 5

*Fred Booth
Minmienadji*

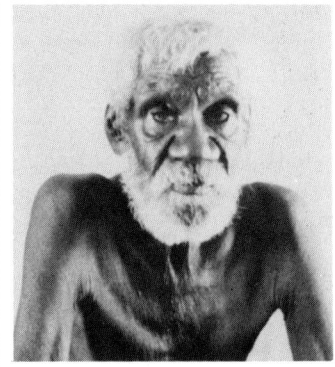

The wild blackfeller. Oh, shot him half a hundred. Just about night-time. One bastard run away. I shot him on the leg. Fall arse over head.

'Where's some blackfellow?' old sergeant said [?] . . .

'I shot one feller over here, crawl about on his knee. I must have broken his knee.'

'Oh good. Where's 'nother fellers?'

'I shot him in the bloody head.'

'Oh, he's in the creek I think.'

Old sergeant look round,

'Oh yeah, here's one bastard shot.'

He was crawl fast round to get up, you know. Sergeant put a gun on him.

They look round.

'One down in the creek?'

Look round,

'Oh he's dead, that feller.'

I shot him on the neck, right here you see.

You were a police tracker?

No! We drovers!

When you shot those fellers, what do you do then?

Burn him. Make a big fire. Burn him.

'Set the fire on him,'

policeman said, sergeant,

'Set some fire on him.'

To burn. They no good.

How many fellers in the fire?

Oh about fifteen. Fifteen blackfellers.

Proper wild ones?

Yeah wild ones mate. No good, they kill you quick.

If you saw some wild feller, like he might be walking along, he didn't see you, would you still shoot him or wait till he threw a spear at you?

Yeah, we can see the bastards a long way 'way.
Yeah we comin' along,
this is blackfeller going along spinifex.

'Oh, there he is!'

[We] Gallopin' over on the horse.

Soon as he jump out and bang!
Finish him.

Tape 1 Side 1

A first encounter with gunfire
Daly Pulkara, Ngarinman, Yarralin

Daly Pulkara and his family

Them bloody whatsa — European come on after that. Banging, banging time now.
They didn't know that. They reckon lightning somewhere. And they reckon,

'Ah, [?] that man he get out bushed.'

They reckon that lightning.

Another bloke drop.

Yeah. Bang! Another bloke drop.

Bang! 'Nother bloke.

The organisation of forces 7

They bin lookin' at, you know, they bin lookin' eye. Something wrong. Got a blood come through the nose.

'Oh might be lightning.'

Bang!
See? They didn't catch on for while. They pick up all the woman and European takem away. Eh? Aborigin just followem up.

Tape 1 Side 1

Keeping watch

Gertie Huddleston Kurrakain, Warndarang, Ngukurr

Ngukurr, near where this incident took place.

Gertie Huddleston Kurrakain describes the period 1880–1910, when the drift of Queensland cattlemen into the Northern Territory was at its peak. The techniques of survival described include hiding in country inaccessible to horses, keeping constant watch and moving into open or watered country only at night.

And they used to sit high up big mountain there, *Walmaja*.

Sometime they used to stay up there now, have look-out boys.
All the [other] ones they go look for lily and cooking, and then boys sing out from top there,

'Somebody coming by horseback!'

They all take off, right on the top of the hill.

They never get them because they were hiding, you know. They tricky too, in the water, they come down in the night for water.

The black trackers used to come on horseback?

Yeah. Not trackers, men from Queensland.

Who paid them, who paid these black policemen?

The White people who brought them up.
Well there was, no, hardly any houses were built, you know, stations, then.

These White men in the station, like at Hodgson Downs, they'd pay these Black police to come and shoot the Mara and Alawa people. Why didn't they do it themselves do you think? Why didn't they go out on horseback and do the shooting?

8   Part One   Chapter One

Because they didn't know where to go, you know.
The native knew where they would hide, you know.
They didn't know where waterholes, too, were.

It seems a bit strange that Aboriginal people should kill Aboriginal people working for White men. Why did they do that, do you think?

Might be, on . . . nothing . . . Might be the White men bin, they told them if they don't do it, they'll shoot them too.
Maybe like that.
I'm just guessing, you know. Unless they were good friends from Queensland times, you know, way back, and they had to do something for their friend.

Tape 1 Side 1

The death of a police tracker

Hickey Hood Janbuyin, Mangarayi, Barunga

Using techniques learned from the official 'native police' of Queensland, the eastern pastoralists employed 'Black trackers' with deadly efficiency. An Alawa man recalled that in the 1930s he had been taught by older people 'never take lollies from a government man and never trust an Aboriginal from Queensland'. To older men and women, 'Queensland boy' (man) is a sinister phrase even today.

Trackers were not always invincible, and Hickey Hood Janbuyin's story illustrates how 'Queensland Jimmy' was outwitted and killed. This man was sent by the pastoralists to invite the bush people to come in for 'a big mob of tobacco', a crude but widely used prelude to massacre.

One Queensland boy called Jimmy, he bin get killed.
Blackfeller killem.

The police planned an ambush:

They [police] want him [Jimmy] go down, go down to blackfellers' camp, you know, longa camp. Well they want go down, makem friend, you know, and tell a lie. He want to tellem lie.

'We're giving you mob tobacco.'

All the [White] people want to try to [make them] go that camp,
all that White men wait there,
gottem gun.

This Jimmy want to takem big mob of [Alawa people]. . .
Jimmy Queensland, takem all this mob, ' ere, Hodgson Down mob, Warliburu [Alawa] blackfeller, trying to takem there, tell lie.

'You want to gettem big mob of tobacco? You likem tobacco?'

But all these fellers bin no more know tobacco [did not yet know about tobacco]. Nobody bin know tobacco. We bin know that after, this tobacco comin'. That nikki-nikki tobacco.

The organisation of forces

So they followed this Jimmy?

Yeah. They didn't want to followem.

This man name Pidgin talking like this mob eh. They know, they talk in the language, you know, this 'nother man [*Pidgin*] tellem this man here,

'Gettem spear. Killem this [*Queensland Jimmy*] man!'

After a time the Whites came to investigate why Queensland Jimmy had not returned.

Well this [*White*] mob coming then, firem shot, want to shootem all this blackfeller, wild blackfeller.
All these whitefellers go that place again, same place where Jimmy bin get killed, and 'nother lot, 'nother lot White men want to try to shoot all this mob here.

They couldn't shootem. They [*the Alawa*] bin get up longa high hill. They runaway.

They didn't shootem.
Missed them.
Missed them.
Missed them all the way.

Who told you that story?

My father.

Tape 1 Side 1

A hill-top ambush

Hoppy Tommy Wanindyulgari, Alawa, Nutwood Downs Station

This story describes another successful Aboriginal attack upon an overlanding party. Evidently the ambushers were completely successful, though what retribution may have followed is unknown.

The account alternates between the general and the particular. The phrase 'want to', used several times in the first part of the story, means 'used to'. For instance, Hoppy Tommy Wanindyulgari means that it was common for ambushers to sit on a hill overlooking the overlanders' track waiting to ambush them. The end of the story, however, relates to a specific event.

The overlanders try to lure a bushman from the hilltop:

They bin do that all this way too, this part.

They bin alda [*always used to*] spearem Queensland boy, before, wild time.

White man bin always shooting behind time.
That [*Aboriginal*] man longa top now, longa hill. Another [*White*] man bin

The grave of one of the hundred or more Whites speared by Aborigines in the Northern Territory.

want to sing out la *[to]* him,

'Hey, you come down, you come down.' *[yelled the Overlander]*
That allabout people there, you know, longa top.

'Oh, I'm right!' *[replied one of the Aborigines from the top of the hill]*

Keep quiet longa top. Longa hill, you know.
Oh, they bin want to findem like that. Good place, you know.

'Right, gimme that rifle now mate.' *[said the overlander]*

That's his mate,

'Gimme rifle.'

He bin givit .They bin look longa him.They bin look like.
He *[the bushman]* want to tease him you know, that blackfeller now, that Queensland boy.

'Ah, I'm right mate. I won't get killed.'

And they bin have big high hill there too, you know, longa top, some people, black native.

'All right, we'll fire a shot longa allabout.' *[said the overlander]*

And they *[bush people]* bin takem big rock longa him, biggest rock they bin chuckem down longa him.
Man and him, they're gone.

Smash up.
Makem mince.
That big stone bin mincem up him.

Finish.

The bush people kill a survivor and take the equipment:

Well this man, 'nother Queensland boy, oh, goin' on they bin killem him, got a spear.
Killem one feller horse. Rope cuttem him now, slingem him. Got a spear, this way through. And horse bin gone. Got the saddle.

That's olden days. They bin want to killem.

The organisation of forces 11

What hill that one?

This way, that's Minimere River way.
And they bin really killem horse and man. And they cuttem that saddle. Leather, you know. That sort of flap they bin want to cuttem, puttem longa arm this way, this way *[like bracelets]*.
And rifle they bin want to havem now. Handy one now. Bullet allabout.

Well that man bin want to come up. One feller Queensland boy they bin puttem . . . bullet. They bin takem bullets longa him. True!

Did they know how to use that rifle?

No, they usem like a woomera. *[They didn't know]* how to usem bullet. They never bin know how to usem rifle.
Think him go off meself.

Tape 1 Side 1

A massacre at Hodgson Downs

Chicken Gonagun and Sandy Mambookyi, Alawa, Hodgson Downs

Left: Chicken Gonagun

Right: Sandy Mambookyi

In 1902 the Eastern and African Cold Storage Supply Company took up some 57,000 square kilometres of the Arnhem Land coast around Blue Mud Bay for use as a cattle run. In 1904, after two bad years, the company took up more land, including Hodgson Downs. It is probably in this period that the story occurred.

This story is reproduced with minor variations, in Alawa, in L. Hercus and P. Sutton (editors): **This is what happened: Historical Narratives by Aborigines** *(pp.177–181.) It also was corroborated by the bushman George Conway, who told a researcher that the Company employed two gangs of ten to fourteen Aborigines, headed by a White man or 'part-Aboriginal', to hunt and kill any Aboriginal on sight.*

The two men who told this story pointed to a spot very close to the present Hodgson Downs Station where this massacre took place.

Chicken Gonagun:
Blackfeller bin want to campin' here, somewhere.

12   Part One   Chapter One

Sandy Mambookyi:
Yeah somewhere, I don't know where. Might be here, I think.

Chicken Gonagun:
Might be here, might be 'long river. Well they [*White men*] bin sendem word, one boy, bin go, tellem allabout:

'Come on, you fellers want to cuttem wood. Boss wantem you fellers.'

I don't know what boss belonga old feller name. Some feller bin bringem up all the way now. They bin takem, bringem down, they givit axe, longa allabout.

'You fellers go cuttem wood.'

Takem allabout, and showem. They bin takem longa that road now where that little gully, you know, little creek. Bailey Creek . . .

Sandy Mambookyi:
Yeah, right along highway now.

Chicken Gonagun:
They bin cuttem wood there now. All the way, you alda [*always*] look that short wood, all about him, stand up coolibah. That one now they bin want to cuttem.

Sandy Mambookyi:
Coolibah they bin cuttem.

Chicken Gonagun:
Cuttem round there, ah, heapem up. Some feller chuckem him, and some feller cuttem and some feller chuckem him in there, heapem up.

They [*the White men, meanwhile*] bin gettem horse now this mob. All the White men bin gettem horse and they bin puttem saddle, saddlem up, greasem rifle.

Sandy Mambookyi:
Snider rifle, I think.

Chicken Gonagun:
Olden times they bin usem, olden times. We bin want to look. They bin usem you know, when we bin little boy.

They bin greasem, some feller horse come on. They bin just go stringin' longa here. Hid behind, you know, one way.

'You fellers see that man now, he comin?' [*asked one of the Aboriginal woodchoppers*]

'We're going to get shot here.'

'No, he only just come up look,'

another old man talk longa that 'nother old man. He talk longa,

'No, he only just come look this firewood, where we gottem, how much wood we gottem.'

'No, he's going to shootem we.'

The Alawa see the Whites approaching to kill them:

They bin see-em:

'You bin see-em that rifle, where they gottem?'

He talk like that, 'nother old man.

They bin just come up roundem up, poor fellow.

'Ah, heapem up there, one side longa wood!'

Like that now, that wood bin like that.
And they bin stand up cross like that, they bin puttem altogether now.

Like that, all the way, right round.

Yeah.

One horse there, two horse here, two horse here, right round.
Round that wood jammem up.

'Now!'

boss bin talk longa allabout.

'Fire!'

Nothing.

When the Whites opened fire, one of the horses placed behind the prisoners to prevent escape was hit. As it reared up, it allowed, briefly, a gap to form through which three men escaped:

One old boy bin hittem one feller horse, right longa face, hittem nose I think, and givit room. And two [prisoner] boy bin get up, and one boy bin get up that way.

See that hill over there? Long way. They bin shootem allabout.

Finishem off.

They bin afterem two-feller man [who had escaped]. Bin afterem that two boy bin jump out like that, here. They bin shootem all right. They bin catchem one feller, right here they bin shootem.

Some feller die allabout, old people, you know, bin shootem there.

'All right. I bin get shot you know. Watchem meself.'

14   Part One   Chapter One

The place where the bodies were burnt.

He bin tellem that 'nother bloke.

That old boy bin beatem allabout longa creek, right here longa Bailey Creek now. He jump down there. He bin gettem run, blackfeller, all round this hill. Walk longa this hill now all the way.

This 'nother one, belonga Nipper father, they bin takem, they bin takem longa that six mile. See that hill? Two men bin afterem, shootem all the way. He just run all the way, him walk. Two feller [*two White men*] just galloping along, eh.

Now then, 'nother one givit along him, he fire longa him, and him [*the escapee*] jump.

'Nother one givit longa him, longa him jump. Two feller loadem up again.

And him walk all the way. They bin give him. Long way, that, eh? Still beatem two-feller.

'All right, old man, you can go away. We got no bullet now.'

Poor bugger, blackfeller.

Were they White men or Queensland boys, chasing?

No. White men, White men.

They bin burnem up, finish.

They bin wait, they bin burn, finish.

And they bin go.

Who told you that story? The story of how they caughtem with the horses like that, who told you that story?

Sandy Mambookyi:
Oh, just people, now eh, different people like that.
People bin runaway eh? That's the man bin takem story now. All over.

Chicken Gonagun:
Tellem everybody, and where we bin born, well, they bin tellem that man about, now.

Did the White men ever shoot those women and children then, and piccaninnies?

The organisation of forces 15

Sandy Mambookyi:
Yes.
Hittem. Killem. Same way they killem, killem longa stick. Gottem stick, knockem in the head or neck.
Some kid, piccanin', that small one, like a goanna, hittem longa tree.

Chicken Gonagun:
Bashem longa stone, chuckem longa stone, or killem.
Might be too cruel. No, just bashem.
You know, too small to shootem, too small.

Sandy Mambookyi:
Women bin run-away, they roundem up, shootem.

Why did they do that, I wonder, do you know?

Chicken Gonagun:
I dunno.
Oh, they bin like to killem, finishem up tribe. Take all of their country.

Sandy Mambookyi:
Might be they want to takem this place, you know, this country.

Tape 1 Side 1

Revenge at Elcho Island

Stephen Bunbaijan, Liyagalawumirr, Galiwin'ku

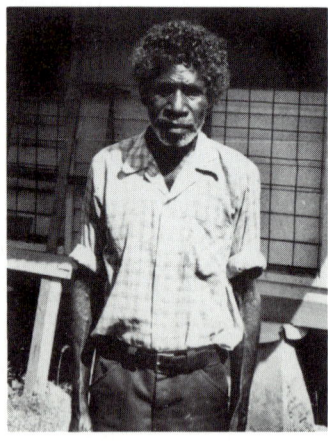

Stephen Bunbaijan

Until about 1907, Macassans from Sulawesi used to visit the north coast to gather trepang (beche de mere), later sold to the Chinese as a delicacy.

In this story, the Macassans used some Aboriginal sacred string to make fishing nets and in reprisal the Aborigines murdered the crews except for a boy who was protected by the speaker's great-grandfather.

Relations with the Macassans seem to have generally been harmonious, so events like the following were probably rare:

I know this story is about my grandfather's father.
Once a Macassan would come, you know, every time they used to come round sailing from Macassan to Arnhem Land coast.

Well, the time when they came back from east, sailing back to home, they anchored round other side. A lot of people, you know.
A lot of our people kill those we have from two boats, and they destroy all of the crews and captains.

Kill those Macassans?

16 Part One Chapter One

Modern Macassan prau similar to the ones used by the Macassans in this story. (Photograph: C.C. MacKnight)

So they . . . and my grandfathers save one young boy.

Why would they kill them?

My father used to tell me, it was for ceremony, traditional string. They used that string, only small string, and they [the Macassans] take it out and tried to make a net for catching [fish].
Then that's why, when those Macassans — that's why they killed them because of their string.

What happened to the little boy? What happened to him?

He tried to run away, you know. Hid into the mangroves, surrounded by mangroves, and my grandfather chase him, just grab by hair. He told him:

'I'll not harm you, I'm not going kill you, I'll try to save you. And when Macassan come back from their home next year, well, I can tell them, and you'll be the witness, so, because, because I didn't start up the trouble. The other people, you saw another people [were] starting up the trouble.'

And convinced him, so my grandfather and his father didn't start up the trouble. They like Macassan, they were friends.

That little boy, did he stay with your father's tribe?

So what happen: and the little boy used to stay with them, and camp around, you know. They used to feed him sugarbag, turtle and everything they had. And the fish too.

When the times Macassan came back from their country, and sailing back this way, so they was still wondering, the Macassans themselves they were still wondering, what was happened for that two boats.

The bay at Galiwin'ku where the Macassans landed.

When they came back they anchored here.

This place here?

Yeah.

Then they, you know, everybodies was hiding, because they know they are the [guilty] tribe, hiding themselves somewhere up the hill here.

Some people think the

The organisation of forces 17

Macassans will kill them.

But the other people, tribe, from Yalukal tribe and others from mainland, Howard Island — some of them, you know, been hiding themselves somewhere.
But others just go down, and because they want tobacco, or whisky or something, or flours, or rice.

So my grandfather, and two of my grandfathers, they were hiding along, you could see the creek, at the side of the creek. See the green leaves?

And when the Macassans came ashore and they come up you know, they just come out and see if they would meet them. And they *[Stephen Bunbaijan's grandfather was]* with the Macassan, the young Macassan.

But the Macassan come ashore, well, they carry guns and knife and everything. Dressed, dressed themselves as soldiers.
So they saw them come down the beach, and Macassan start pointing up a gun just towards them and my grandfather's not frightened. And because the Macassan man he said:

'All of you no frightened because I'm here. Well, I think you'll be saved. The others will be killed.'

So they all come down and met them.
But they still pointing up — the gun to them, you know, and what they told him. They asked the young Macassan a lot of questions, and he told them what had happened.
And all right, they proved, you know, they believed *[the great grandfather]* because they saw that young Macassan.

He was a witness?

They hear from him, also they saw he's still alive.

[The Macassan boy said:] 'If you want to kill these people, how about kill me, because these people are save my life. The others not, I know the others, but at least this family are safe now.'

From there they move away, long way, maybe say a quarter of a mile *[400 metres]* and there they have the little court, you know, they still have that court. But the Macassans said 'no' but my grandfather tell Macassan,

'How about you could take me to Macassan as a prisoner?'

Well, Macassan said:

'All right, I take you, but still remember what I'll do. I'll still kill these *[other]* people, then I'll be satisfied. Including you, I'll take you prisoner for three years. All right. Then *[in]* Arnhem Land these people will be free. No fighting anymore.'

Not recorded on accompanying tape

A massacre at Mirki

Anon, Milingimbi

Transcribed from Gupapuyngu by Gularranga in 1976, edited by Matjarra and translated by Michael Christie.

This event occurred near Murwangi (Florida Station), eighty kilometres south-west of Milingimbi. The Station was taken up in 1885 and abandoned a few years later.

Some time later, according to another Milingimbi man, Florida Station was taken up again by Billy Farrer. He was forced to abandon the Station in the 1930s because of Aboriginal attacks upon the cattle.

The events in this story are:
1. *Some Whites met two Aboriginal women and learned the whereabouts of the camp, at Mirki.*
2. *An Aboriginal confessed to cattle killing, and was murdered.*
3. *The adults at Mirki were murdered in a surprise night attack.*
4. *The surviving children were murdered on the following day.*

More people came on horses.

'Hey! Let's go and have a look on the plains over there. We'll go and see if we can find some of the Aboriginal people cooking on the plains over there.'

And they went, with ten horses. They went, and they came out on to the plains at Dhamala, and they went round the edges, and right into the middle. They kept going, then: two women.

'Look! There! There! There! There! Someone's coming!'

The women were coming from getting shellfish and crabs. They rode up to them and quickly met them.

'Where do you live?'

Like that.

'Over there.'

That's what the two women said.

'At Mirki.'

'At Mirki?'

'Yeah.'

'Where's that?'

'In the jungle.'

'Oh, all right. We're just asking. That's good. And where are you going now?'

'Over there to Mirki. That is the place called Mirki, there.'

And back the stockmen went. They galloped back to Murwangi. At Murwangi:

'It's true, those Aboriginals are eating our cattle. Some of the women told us. We met two of the women.'

'Where are they?'

'I suppose they're in the jungle where they said they live.'

'Good. Later on we'll go and fight them. We'll go over there on our horses.'

That's what the enemies said, the *Balanda [White men]* enemies.

Well they took their horses, about ten of them, the same ones. Off they went, first to Yathalamara. And from Yathalamara, to Dunu. At Dunu they saw something.

'What's that?'

They were just on to the clear grassy plains and they had seen a man.

'There! There's an old man.'

Like that. Up they galloped.

'Hey, who are you?' they said.

'I'm me.'

'Oh. You people are the ones who steal our horses. Right?'

'Yes,' he said.

'Cattle, you steal them too?'

'Yeah!'

'Okay, how many at a time do you eat?'

'Lots and lots and lots and lots, we always spear your cattle.'

'Okay, where are you going now?'

'I'm going over to Mirki,' said the man.

One of the stockmen said,

'Okay, off you go. You can go now.'

And this is what he did. He turned around, and those stockmen shot him in the back with their guns.
Right away, dead, by those guns.

Well, he was just stretched out in the plains and they left him.

'Come on, let's go back.'

So they went back to Murwangi. They arrived.

'We've killed one Aboriginal, he's lying out there somewhere.'

'Serves him right,' said the boss to them. 'Serves him right. Where are they all?'

'Well,' he said, 'they were in the jungle. We're just off there now.'

Up they got, galloped away, and it was night. Through the night they galloped and arrived at Mirki, spreading out to surround the place. Surrounding, meeting around the other side.

In the jungle at Mirki, and there they heard something: they heard the people playing the *djunggirriny* ceremony. Didgeridoo, clapsticks, dancing, in the jungle.

'They're dancing right here!'

Like that.

'They must have come here into the jungle. Good,' they said.

'Hey we'd better watch out for ourselves; some of those bad White people might come from Murwangi,' the Aboriginal people said to themselves, 'but we will look after each other, won't we?'

'Yes, we'll keep a look out, because it's dark now. We'll go out and have a look all through the jungle.'

Like that.

But when they went, they saw the horses, surrounding them completely.

Only the horses, the White men had got off their horses and were standing up. The Aboriginals stood there and looked at the Europeans. The Europeans could not see them.

One of them said,

'There's a lot of them, isn't there?'

The horses were standing all around. There, at Mirki, in the jungle, that's where they were.
And when the men returned to the people, they questioned them.

'Where are they all?'

'What, the enemies? Here. We're all here together, Whites and Aboriginals.'

'What did you see?'

'We saw all those horses. What are we going to do? How are we going to escape?'

'We can't escape, we're just going to have to wait here and see what happens. They will soon arrive here,' said one old Aboriginal man. 'Lots and lots and lots of them. What will we do? We'll have to stay here at Mirki. We won't be able to get away, but the jungle will hide us.'

Then,

'What will we do?'

'I don't know. What will we do? Maybe we can all climb up into the trees, up in a tree we can all sleep, we'll stay up in a tree all the time.'

'And all the children?'

'All the children will be put up into a tree too. We can all stay up in the trees. First we'll make a shelter up there.'

So they all lay up in the trees. They climbed up, all of them, into a tree. Into a tree they climbed, all of them. They sat there, they didn't say anything, nothing. They were very careful for each other.

The White men arrived, and went into the thick jungle area. They entered, and stood there.

'This is their place, where did they go?'

'Ah, there they are!'

'Ah, yes!'

And the rest of them arrived, and more as well. A lot of them, enemies arrived, yes, enemies. Yes, and they all stood around, where the pond is.

'Where are they?'

'Here they are. They've all climbed up into these trees.'

Then they said:

'We'll shoot at them. Straight up into the trees.'

One stood here, one stood there, one stood there. Think about the noise that those guns made, shooting up into the trees.
Shooting, shooting, shooting, up into the trees.
They all fell down into the ground, and just lay there all over the ground, every one of them, until they were all dead.

But one of them was still alive. The horses had passed him on the way there. He saw them, and he hid in the cycad palms, underneath them. It might have been cycads or pandanus, something like that.

'These bushes are thick. I will be down here so that while they are shooting at them, I will stay alive,' he said.

His name, the child who as hiding, was Ditjarama . . .
And he hid all by himself .

So they shot at them until they were all dead, and in the morning they came back again, and found nothing. They were all lying dead. They left them there, all adults, and off they went.
They talked about it with their boss.

'Serves them right. How many did you kill?'

'There must have been a hundred of them. Hiding up in the trees.'

'We shot at them into the trees, and they all came falling down.'

'Lots and lots of them.'

Well, they slept, there at Murwangi.

The boss:

'I think I'll go and see them.'

Maybe he was feeling sorry, but then again, maybe he wasn't. But anyway, off he went. He wanted to go by himself, just the boss.
Off he went, and there he saw a lot of children, just like the ones we've got at Milingimbi school, boys and girls, just like that he saw them all, they were playing. Up he rode. He tied up his horse, and went over and met them.

'Hey, it's me!'

Like that. The children were all very happy.

Then,

'Come on, come on, come on. Gather round me here. I'm a nice man. I'm just like you are,' he said. 'Good. I won't do anything to you.'

And the children stood there.

'Hey children. Wait. Just a minute! How many of you are there?'

Like that.

So the children lined up, and stood in two straight lines.
How many?
Two, two lines. Just like soldiers do.

One line here, one line there, two of them.

And the White man stood in front of them.

'Now you watch me,' he said. 'Watch me carefully, and look at this, it's my spear.'

You see he had a repeater rifle, one which fires a lot of bullets. That's what he had, that White man.

'You watch me carefully! Just watch me. Don't look anywhere, keep your eyes on me.'

And he pulled the trigger, I think.

And they all just went falling down onto the ground. Every one of them, just lying there, and not only a few, lots of them.

Children, just like we have here at school, girls and boys. All those children just like our ones here at Milingimbi.

Tape 1 Side 1 | A baby's life saved at the Elsey

Jess Roberts Garalnganjag and Maudie Munguj, Mangarayi, Jilkminggan

Not all encounters were as murderous as the two previous stories suggest. In this account, the Whites surprised the Mangarayi living on Elsey Station as they camped beside the Roper River. In their haste to escape they forgot about a baby, Maudie Manguj's mother, who was still in her coolamon (bark carrying basket). The baby was not only spared but moved into the shade.

The comparatively late date of this story (perhaps 1910), as well as the event itself, suggests that the Whites intended to frighten the bush people away from the station area rather than kill them.

Jess Roberts Garalnganjag:
When you bin little kid . . .

Maudie Manguj:
Yuwayi *[yes]*.

Jess Roberts Garalnganjag:
They used to runaway too, gottem you mob, ain't it?

Maudie Manguj:
Yuwayi. They used to leavem, got a coolamon again, my mother.
Yeah, they bin just jump in *[the river]* and leavem me. Good job *na-yijar na-whitefeller [it was a good job that the White man who found her was a good man]*.

Jess Roberts Garalnganjag:
Your mother, bin leavem you, got a coolamon longa bank.

Maudie Manguj:
Yuwayi. She gone, longa water.

Tu! Tu! Tu! Tu! Tu! Tu!

Jess Roberts Garalnganjag:
Firem shot everywhere.

You know that White man bin pickem up that olgooman [old woman] when he [she] bin longa coolamon.
Pickem up him and him bin puttem out of the river bank and puttem him longa whannim [whatsaname] now, longa palm tree, you know.
That White man bin pickem up that old lady, puttem longa coolamon, puttem in longa palm tree, you know like shade, you know. And just leave it im like that. Till mother and father gonna come back, and pickem up.

No, they never killem. Just leave it like that.

Maudie Manguj:
Another man he bin want to killem me.

Jess Roberts Garalnganjag:
And [the baby's] his mother and father come back again and look around for him, and they still findem in 'nother place you know.

Tape 1 Side 1

An execution in the Roper Valley

Gertie Huddleston Kurrakain, Warndarang, Ngukurr

Left:
Northern Territory Times and Gazette, 28 December 1894

Right:
Northern Territory Times and Gazette, 25 January 1895

If there is no other satisfaction to be derived from the purposed hanging of the blackfellow Moolooloorun it will at least wipe out for the time being that ghastly blemish on our constitution of keeping a prisoner waiting six months for his fate. This blackfellow was sentenced to death on the 8th of August, and he has been ironed in gaol ever since. Within a week of his sentence he was probably forgotten by everyone but his gaolers, and there was never the slightest intention on the part of anyone to appeal on his behalf. At his trial he was practically self convicted, and when a prisoner confesses his guilt all avenues leading to an appeal may be considered to be blocked. In such a case if hanging is to be done at last it seems harsh and unmerciful to keep the doomed man manacled in prison for half a year waiting to know what the white man proposes to do with him next. Serious persons who have had much experience of our courts know that the average trial of natives is a weird farce. The conventional forms and ceremonies are carried out with care and precision, but for all that the native knows about them the court might just as well be dealing with a block of wood. The farce is not ended until the wretched creatures are made to wait six months for the final act. Is it not time that we made an earnest endeavour to introduce a system with less of an air of brutality about it?

In 1894 a Chinese was murdered near Crescent Lagoon on Elsey Station, and in accordance with current policy, the man found guilty, Moolooloorun, was executed at the scene of the crime.

Moolooloorun, the condemned native, was duly hanged at Crescent Lagoon on the 17th instant, and Mr. Little and his party are now on their way home again. Particulars are not yet to hand, except so far as to state that death was instantaneous. No doubt the Deputy-Sheriff feels more contented in mind now than he had done for a week or two previous to the execution. There is no comfort to be derived from a duty which compels you to travel a journey of 300 miles with a murderer in tow for the purpose of hanging the convicted one at a specified time on a specified date; and in wet weather, too, when annoying delays might occur any day. Then, besides weather condition, there was also the possibility —a vague one, perhaps, — of the prisoner escaping, or of the hangman deserting. As, however, none of these disasters overtook the party, and as the convict was executed in the most approved style, the Deputy-Sheriff should return to his headquarters in a fine state of mental complacency after his 600-mile journey.

The organisation of forces 25

Gertie Huddleston Kurrakain believes that organised resistance ceased after this event. If the intention of the Whites was to make a dramatic gesture, they succeeded, for this story is one of the most commonly told in the Roper Valley.

Yeah, well, the only way the native will know it's wrong, you know, to do murder.
So they go and bring all them people from all over the places, different tribes, everywhere. They have big meeting and they had this, they had this hole dug. They told them,

'No killing White people any more, because you'll, they'll do the same to you.'

They hang him on the tree, in front of everybody.

After that, they, you know, settle down a bit then.

I never heard anybody since hanging of that old man, murdering more people, White people.

Attack and counter attack at Bowgan Station

Tape 1 Side 1

Jack Cotton Mobalily, Wambaya, Brunette Downs

By 1910 Aborigines in the pastoral districts were learning not to attack Whites indiscriminately, for the consequences were too severe. Attacks were confined to particular White men for particular misdeeds. Many bush people now had relatives living and working at the stations. The pastoralists also mounted 'punitive expeditions' more commonly in pursuit of certain individuals rather than all the bush people.

This story is set on the Barkly Tableland, probably before 1920. By this time the pastoralists were already in control of most of the area, for the open gidgee and grasslands, ideal horse country, gave little protection for the bush people.

The stages of the story described by Jack Cotton Mobalily are:
1. *A white yard-builder found in bed with an Aboriginal woman was killed by her husband.*
2. *The body was discovered by Jack Berry, the station lessee, and a 'punitive expedition' planned. The pastoralists agreed to start shooting at a certain time, except for Harry Bates of Eva Downs Station, who would take no part in it.*
3. *The 'tail' (mainly older women) of one fleeing Aboriginal group, was caught by the Whites and shot.*
4. *Some of the sons of the mothers shot by Berry's party killed Berry.*

When Jack Berry was living there [at Bowgan] there was a big mob of people there then, you know . . . all blackfellers, woman, man. He's got along all right with these people. Used to talk to 'em, one or two language, some people.

26 Part One Chapter One

And there long time, and he got on all right, and the people got on all right with him.

And he had a yard-builder. He wasn't a carpenter, according to me old grandfather, he was a yard-builder.
Of course there was no house to be built in them days. He was old yard-builder.
Then he wanted a woman.
I don't know how he got this woman, well, the woman went over and camped with him.

And he [*her husband*] wait too long for this woman to come back. This is what the grandfather tell me, and when this feller went up, he went to that yard, and he heard this feller in bed with her — this feller. That's why he killed this [*yard-builder*] feller now.

Killed him in the bed.

Took the woman away.
Coverem over with his own blanket.
Left him there.

Jack Berry, he was away,
doing some mustering, way east. He had to camp out for a couple of days.
And when he came back . . . he told the boys,

'I'll ride ahead,'

to bloke bringing the pack horse along,

'I'll go ahead.'

Funny, he got back home at old Bowgan. You know, he couldn't see where this feller, whether the feller still lived with him or dunno, he couldn't see any fire or fresh turn-out, nothin', you know, somethin'.
It was only old Jack Berry and he only had a little fuckin' humpy then.

And he looks round a bit, he goes to where, and goes over to the yard, and he's . . . that where he found him — dead.

I don't know what happened, whether . . . I think . . . he had to write a letter to the policeman at Anthony [*Lagoon*].
Policeman come there, and I think they buried him.

Then — they start to make up their mind there now, before they done all this shooting.
They had to tell all the other people, you know, so they all start [*shooting*] same time. They didn't start shooting there theirself. But they all started the same time. According to this old man was telling me.
See, they had to [*get*] permission to start off shooting, so they all start same time.

Of course, it's a . . . Eva Downs, old Harry Bate was there. He told 'em:

'I won't shoot here and don't come and shoot here! Let the people all off here.'

So, well, they must have start shootin'.

Well, those people must have been still campin' up the river there.

Some of them might have got a bit frightened, and went a bit further somewhere. When the feller got killed. But not too far away.
And when the shooting started, they start to follow them people now, Jack Berry and his people, workin' men he had. This bloody fuckin' *[unidentified]* was with him , I think, and . . .
. . . they could only find the tail.
All the old ladies couldn't run fast enough.
Well, those few ladies, mother of this mob, he's got.

I don't know how they did it, they didn't seem to have any power to stop him, stop this feller *[one of Jack Berry's men]*.
Might have had a policeman, too, this feller, Jack Berry feller. Might, but I don't know.
See?

So they shottem, shot all these old ladies.
Shottem.
Keep further on and they were shootin' all the way along up the river then.

But this string of blackfeller went bush, you know, and this old feller that was telling me the story, he was a small boy, this old man. He was with the lead, with his father. He got to Eva Downs.

It must have took 'em few days to get there, but they got to Eva Downs.

That's why they never get shot, that mob. Old Harry Bate told them not to shoot any people here, and don't come here to shoot. He saved the bloody mob there. Thousands of them. That's the story the old man told me.

After this shooting they must have settled.
See?
The mob got away to Eva Down, and they shot a mob, and burnem, and they start to settle.

He *[Jack Berry]* still had this *[unidentified]* man working for him. Then the mob of people must have think about,

'I think we'll have to kill this man, *[who]* kill our mother.'

That was after the shooting.

And then they shot him, see,
Shot him in the night.
See where he's — he's in a little humpy — see where this gun is standing.
He's sleep with his door open.
They must have, then they got bullet . . . first, when they was workin in daytime, they got bullet, in there, that bullet, hide. Then he had no trouble to sneak up and get that gun.

Tape 1 Side 1 | **The death of Brigalow Bill**

Daly Pulkara, Ngarinman, Yarralin

Daly Pulkara recounting the story of Brigalow Bill.

'Brigalow Bill' Ward established a station a few kilometres from the present Humbert River Homestead in about 1908. He was murdered the following year. According to Daly Pulkara, Brigalow Bill was killed because he had shot at or killed some Ngarinman people. His death was engineered with the co-operation of one of the women working for him, who stole his gun. Another account, taken down by a policeman at Timber Creek Police Station soon after the murder, is reproduced here also. This account largely tallies with Daly Pulkara's, except for the insistence that the plans were drawn up by the woman herself.

The stages of Daly Pulkara's story are:
1. Brigalow Bill moved to the Humbert River area and fired at some Ngarinman people.
2. Some months later, these people moved near to Ward's camp. Some of them asked one of the women working there to hide his revolver in the billycan when next she fetched water.
3. Brigalow Bill, powerless to prevent the attack, was speared and buried in a shallow grave on the river bank.
4. The police wrongly arrested Daly Pulkara's uncle. Meanwhile the real culprit, Gordon, was shot by a police tracker.

Brigalow Point: to the north where Brigalow was killed. (Photograph: Debbie Rose, 1980)

Brigalow come here, all the VRD *[Victoria River Downs]* bin start, put up. Then he tried to come up here and put up another station here. Yeah . . . and Brigalow.

And he had that girl with him?

Yeah.
And there's 'nother mob. He *[Brigalow]* went up to the river here called Riley's Pocket, you know, and he find 'nother mob there, that Aborigin mob. He firin', all run away from him.

[Some time later] And that mob come round here, and they find the place for him,

'Oh, he got a place up here.'

He got the two girl then, took one after that firing, walk around with him.

And all this people they call,

The organisation of forces 29

people call Kungurlulu River, that part of people now, and they follow him all the way down, trackem over the horse then.

Come and make camp. They didn't nearly, oh, might be three months now, three months or two months, makin' a camp.
And they come out here, climb up this hill and hill, and they went up there to see two or three girl, go down the river, you know, with a billycan.
They went up there, sneak round and askem.

[The woman said:] 'Oh, we working with this old feller.'

'He too cheeky?'

'Yeah, I think he's too cheeky by the way he's firin'!
Bang! Bang! Bang!
Might be cheeky all right.'

'How many rifle *[revolver]* he got?'

'He got only one rifle.'

'All right. When you come up next time, come down here get some water, and you can bring that rifle with you.'

And that woman walk out for water and get that revolver and put it in the billycan and go down to river, and givit to them bloke.
And then man just *[said]* 'Come out' — calling old Brigalow. Nearly six o'clock, I think, half an hour. And old Brigalow went up to toilet, and they take the revolver away, you see, into the river.

Brigalow come out and just look round for his rifle.
Nothing there.
He couldn't do nothing.
Give up.
And he couldn't ask that woman where the rifle. He's too late.

Lot of them people just comin' in, straight into it. Spearem right place, in his heart.
Soon as he get one spear, and he fall back, lot of spearses, get in every way, he couldn't fall down.
Spear everywhere, and hold him up in a balance!

Sit down like this.

They get him right out and takem down the river, and buryem in the sand, like this, eh? Easy to pick up. Coverem up and put a stone top of that.
They walkin' away, and whatsis . . . policeman called Jardine, I think, Jaradine?
And he come out here, find everything. And he get up that big bloodwood tree, take a photo of that place.

They went around the river, and one old bloke, they call old Riley, he takem to show them where the place, buryem that man.
They diggem out and they get them bone and takem away, takem in the places.

30 *Part One Chapter One*

All the way down in the packhorse. No motor car bin last here, no aeroplane. And they only bin takem in the station, and mailem out from there.

And policeman went up there. I think that man called John, anyway he got a name in the big bottle tree. Gordon, that's the bloke who killed him, Brigalow. He [the policeman] got the wrong two bloke now.

Was it your father that he arrested, took to Darwin?

Yeah. No, uncle. My father's brother.

And they took him off to Darwin?

Yeah. They were moved to Darwin. Keep him there for, I don't know, might be nearly twelve years.
From young time to old.

And he was the wrong man?

Wrong man, yeah.
Well, he didn't have much English talk to White man, you know. He just give up.

Why did the policeman catch him, do you know?

Well, ah, they think he bin kill that old Brigalow.

And who really did do it?

Gordon, Gordon. Yeah. That's the bloke bin get shot right up this Bitter Creek.

End of Tape 1 Side 1

Not recorded on accompanying tape

An eye-witness account of the same event

This version was taken down word for word by Mounted Constable W. Holland and recorded in the Timber Creek Police Station Journal, 17 April 1910.

Topsy:
'A little bit long time after we come back from Bulleta [Station] with tucker one morning me and Brigalow been burn grass close up long a house. Judy and Peecoota sit down close up long a house. Blackfellow big mob come up long a creek. Me and Brigalow run long a house. Blackfellow throwem spear and missem. We go inside house and Brigalow look out him put pistol long a blanket. Him no more find em. Blackfellow him inside house and Windaran kill him long a ribs long a spear all same butcher knife. Big mob blackfellow come long a house and all about kill Brigalow altogether long a spears. Then big fat blackfellow cut Brigalow neck all same bullock. Blackfellow name Ooray. Ooray do that. Another blackfellow no more savee him name then put pack surcingle long a Brigalow and drag him away long a creek. Judy come up then and pull Brigalow whisker and she been say, " Good job me no more been like him". Blackfellow then allabout take em tucker long a house and take em saddle. Longa bush. All about been ride em horse and muster

The organisation of forces

bullock. Blackfellow George been have Brigalow pistol and shootem two-fellow bullocks. Then him been break pistol long a stone and throw em long a creek. Windaran take me long a bush and him take Peecoota too. Him kill Peecoota long a bush Ooray take Judy long a bush. We been start long time long a bush then Windaran him send me and Lily long a Jim Wickham's look out tobacco. We no more been go. We run away long a Charlie Whittaker's place and I been tell em Mrs Whittaker. Lily no more long a bush when blackfellow kill em Brigalow. Judy been tell me longa bush she been plant em blackfellow long a creek and tell him kill Brigalow. She tell me she been plant em Brigalow pistol. She been take it long a bucket and gammon fetch em water longa creek.'

For another account of the death of Brigalow Bill, see D. Rose, **Hidden Histories,** *Aboriginal Studies Press, 1991, pp. 119–129.*

Chapter Two
A homeland deserted: the Coniston Massacre, 1928

Not recorded on accompanying tape

Summary of events

	1924	One of the worst droughts in memory affects the whole of central Australia
	June 1928	Cattle killing by Aboriginals increasing; several White men threatened
	2 Aug 1928	Brooks leaves Coniston Station to trap dingoes
	7 Aug 1928	Brooks killed at Brooks Soak
	13-25 Aug 1928	Murray's patrol 'investigates' Brooks' death
	28 Aug 1928	Morton attacked at Boomerang Waterhole
	29 Aug 1928	Murray arrives in Alice Springs with two men charged with Brooks' murder
	30 Aug 1928	Morton asks for another police party to arrest his attackers
	4 Sept 1928	Second police expedition sets out
	18 Sept 1928	Alice Springs Police Commissioner receives Murray's final report
	30 Dec 1928	Court of Enquiry begins hearings 'Concerning the killing of Natives in Central Australia by Police Parties and others'
	18 Jan 1929	Board of Enquiry finds that 'the shooting was justified'

The Coniston Massacre was the third and last of the official 'punitive expeditions' mounted against the bush people in the Northern Territory. The first, in 1894, followed the spearing of two telegraph officers at Barrow Creek. The second, on the Daly River ten years later, followed the murder of several tin miners. Memories of these first two events are now naturally confused and vague. In 1977, however, memories of the Coniston Massacre were precise, for many of the people who relate the events were eye-witnesses.

Pastoralists occupied the Coniston area from about 1900. There had been violent resistance by Warlpiri and Anmatyerre in the period 1890–1910, followed by an uneasy truce. The guerilla war seemed to be over. Then in 1924 the worst drought in living memory began in central Australia. The cattle drank the waterholes dry, filled in the soaks by trampling and reduced the vegetation upon which the bush people depended.

Cattle killing remained a dangerous business. For forty years the bush people *had been jailed, whipped or shot for killing stock. By the 1920s the older men, at least, were probably prepared to leave them alone.*

As the drought worsened the demand for rations on the stations and missions increased, yet the Whites were finding it more difficult to carry on. Refusal to supply rations caused threats of violence. Randall Stafford, the Coniston manager, was warned that Aborigines from the west were coming in to kill him. In July 1928 he and Moar, the manager of nearby Pine Hill station, asked the Alice Springs police to restore order.

The immediate cause of worsening relations was women. Two men, Fred Brooks and Nugget Morton, had taken Aboriginal women and not returned them to their husbands. The Whites, by the implied agreement, should now supply food, tobacco and material goods to the husband and his relatives. The demands might have grown so great that Brooks and Morton were unable to accommodate them all, but it is more likely that they made little attempt to honour their obligations. Possibly they had only very vague notions what these were.

Brooks was attacked at daybreak on 7 August 1928. His throat was cut and his body bundled into a rabbit hole. On the 28th, two hundred kilometres away, Morton was attacked but his great strength enabled him to fight off his attackers, crawl to his revolver and shoot his way clear. Meanwhile a messenger had been despatched to Alice Springs to announce the death of Brooks. He met the police patrol, led by Mounted Constable William Murray, already riding up-country to answer the request of Stafford and Moar.

Receiving the news that Brooks was dead and Morton injured, Murray may have imagined that the general uprising predicted by some had occurred. He reorganised his expedition: Paddy, his Arrernte tracker, was joined by two others, Major and Dodger. Stafford and two other local bushmen, Saxby and Briscoe, rode together in a party no longer intended simply to investigate. Morton joined the party later, and the other Whites dropped out.

One can only guess at the fear that gripped the heart when a Warlpiri or Arrernte messenger, breathless and shaking, stumbled into the bush camps to cry out that the Whites had begun killing every Aborigine they found. Within a month over one hundred Aborigines were dead. Anguish replaced terror as the echoes of the guns faded. That anguish has never been forgotten, though many Europeans, because they never heard it, thought it had.

The Warlpiri, who carried the worst of the madness of the Whites, and who tell the stories in this chapter, today live in a wide fringe of settlements on the edges of the traditional homelands. Only recently have outstations been established in some of the old living areas. The large settlements of Lajamanu, Wave Hill, Tennant Creek, Alekarenge (Ali Curung) and Yuendumu form a great circle of sanctuaries to which men, women and children fled for their lives in 1928, or to which they were later escorted. Sixty years after the Coniston Massacre many of the elderly still found it too sad to return to the Warlpiri heartland.

The country is still a homeland deserted. The experience of one young survivor who found the dead bodies at Wajinpulungk was that of many others. After the massacre life had to begin again, no longer in the homeland but in the White men's institutions:

'That's it. We keep going and we bin stop round that country now. And grow up. Get young man (become initiated). And we bin find a job, work, and work around. Droving, some feller. And we bin make Phillip Creek (church mission near Tennant Creek).'

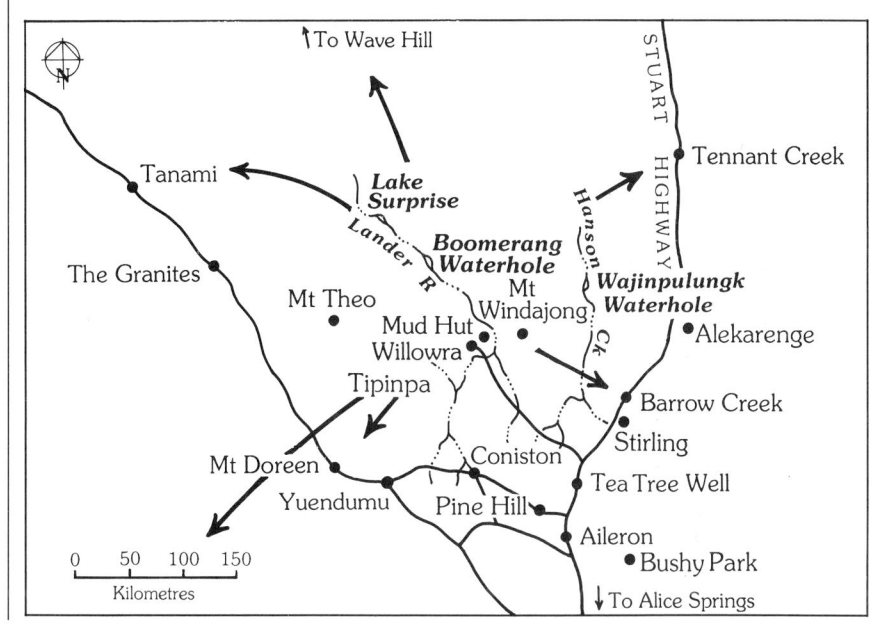

Coniston — the movement of people away from the violence.

Tape 1 Side 2 | The death of Fred Brooks

Blind Alec Jupurrula and Engineer Jack Japaljarri, Warlpiri, Alekarenge

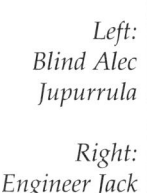

Left: Blind Alec Jupurrula

Right: Engineer Jack Japaljarri

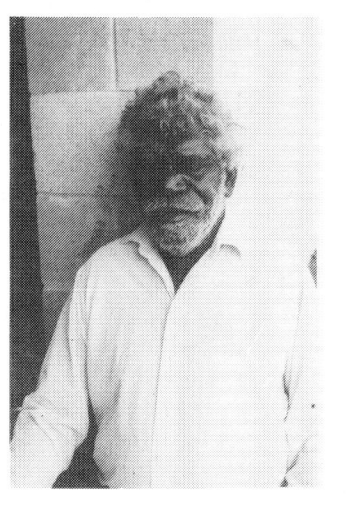

The family of Blind Alec Jupurrula was living near Brooks Soak at the time Brooks was killed. As the police approached the family split up. His mother went to Mount Doreen Station, while Blind Alec Jupurrula fled with his aunt to Wave Hill Station.

He described how Brooks, trapping dingoes, asked one of the men to lend his wife to him for 'washing clothes'. The woman did not return.

A homeland deserted: the Coniston Massacre, 1928 35

Blind Alec Jupurrula:
Freddie in the camp and he askem for that lady, old lady, you know. And he askem that old man:

'Let that woman go washing clothes for me, and *[I'll]* let her go after washing clothes. I'll give you tucker.'

And so old man let her go, that old lady.
That Freddie took him away, washing clothes, but he *[Brooks]* never comin' back. He never comin' back with the tucker. He keepem there, right till . . . watching, all day.

Never coming back, old lady.

Watching half the night, right till, just about daylight he come. Just about the day break. When he come open up.
He come, when he get up, that old Freddie, going to make it fire. And he go back again la *[in]* bed. He's tell that old lady: 'You make a fire!'

And he *[Nugget, the husband]* come close up, that old man, watching all day, and he come watching all night, and he come just about daylight. Waiting. Look for that old lady.

Freddie was in bed.

Engineer Jack Japaljarri:
Married man.

Blind Alec Jupurrula:
Yeah, married man, to that old lady. Old lady went to makit fire.

[Nugget, the husband said:] 'What's that man?' old man asking.

'Where's that man? Where's that whitefeller?'

He askem now. He come out.
He givem a cheek *[hit Brooks]*.
One boomerang he puttem right through here *[indicating throat]* and he cut him with stone knife.

He cuttem with stone knife.
Finish.

You know that Nugget . . .

Engineer Jack Japaljarri:
Bin smart people.

Blind Alec Jupurrula:
Yeah, him smart. You know Nugget . . .

Engineer Jack Japaljarri:
That old man bin really smart you know. He didn't know anything *[European]*, but he used to be really smart people.

Blind Alec Jupurrula:
One half-caste bloke bin there, one half-caste bloke.

Engineer Jack Japaljarri:
One half-caste bloke.

Blind Alec Jupurrula:
Alec.

Engineer Jack Japaljarri:
He's gone back and callem up soldiers now.

Blind Alec Jupurrula:
He called that *[Constable]* Murray, too.

Engineer Jack Japaljarri:
Murrays.

Blind Alec Jupurrula:
Was policeman.

Engineer Jack Japaljarri:
Policeman, Murray.

Blind Alec Jupurrula:
He called big mob soldier. They comin', tracker, its the police boy you know. And soldier, big mob soldier, come and look for that man.

Tape 1 Side 2

The discovery of Brooks' body and the formation of the first police party

Tim Japangardi, Warlpiri, Yuendumu

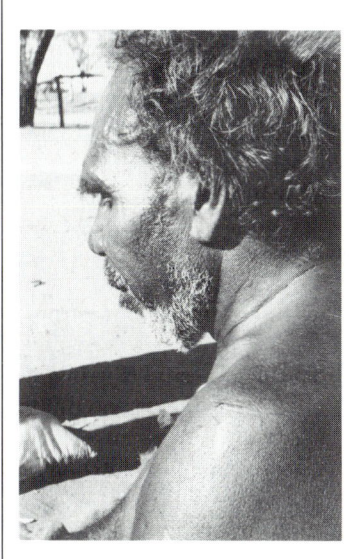

Tim Japangardi

Alec Wilson was travelling with a cattleman, Joe Brown, and two Aboriginal men. Brown was suffering from beri-beri, and died a day before Brooks was killed. The body was stripped ('the two blokes took everything') while Wilson pressed on for Coniston Station. On the way he passed Brooks' Soak, discovered Brooks' body and arrived at Coniston with the news of the death of two Whites.

They was going along on the camel or horses, just the camel and horse I suppose.
And I dunno what Alec reckon.

And then, they pick two old bloke up here longa Mount Doreen, someway, west, doctor man you know.
They brought along, and they was helping them little bit. And Alec left that two old bloke in there with him, you know.

A homeland deserted: the Coniston Massacre, 1928 37

When old man *[Joe Brown]* died, and the two bloke just took everything then, that two old bloke and Alec went on to, till, trying to get on with the police, or Randall Stafford, in Coniston.
When he went by then he saw the dead body, Brooks feller, that was happened, like, yesterday morning. And he got through there about lunch time, I think.

He just discovered it by accident then, just walked by that rabbit hole?

He saw that, what was happening — he didn't see, but, you know, he saw body in the rabbit hole.
Something was buried.
He saw the blood, he saw the piece of boomerang and nulla nullas and all that, with, you know, broken up. What was happening.
And he went on, and he went to Coniston, and told everybody about it.

[The Coniston manager said:] 'Oh, that must be old Fred got killed.'
After that, when he told everybody, oh, the shooting was on then.

Do you remember how the people you were with — somebody must have told them that Fred was dead. Did someone come into the camp and tell you?

Oh, yeah, one bloke. Two old bloke, you know. They got frighten, and they run across the country, and they went over right over on Mount Theo, and tell everybody 'bout:

'Oh, there's big shooting going on down here, that was accident Brooks' Soak. Something about, oh, it must be over women, something.'

They reckon, they told us, that *[White]* people went down there two or three times in the camp with a rifle, and took the wife off them. They might get really angry with him.

We couldn't come *[return]* till about, oh, two or three years.
We still staying there, away from, you know, no water, horse couldn't get drinkin', anywhere at all, was right out of it, right out from waterhole country.

So the first time you heard about Brooks being dead, was when you heard that the shooting had started?

I was still up on Mount Theo. My father went across, you know, he got to make sure, and he ran into them, this people with shooting. That happened to my father too, ran into that mob.

He get shot?

Yeah.

Did he know what it was about? Some fellers didn't even . . .

No no no.
Some of them, they didn't know, you know, what was going on and what was happening, or what for, what for the firing was on.

Too late, then, and that two old bloke come along, and just about shooting was over then, and tell everybody.

'Don't go more, unless everything's over.'

They still firing. We have to, you know, keep move. Still move on to about another thirty miles, to another spring.

Tape 1 Side 2

Murder at Mission Creek

Jimmy Jungarrayi, Warlpiri, Yuendumu

Mission Creek is some twenty kilometres north of Yuendumu. According to Jimmy Jungarrayi, the police search party did not travel much further west than Coniston Station itself. At Mission Creek the police searched the surrounding country, then turned northwards in the direction of Willowra.

Water bin there, that way, water, creekwater.
Runnin' this way.
Might be there.
Big conkerberry there, somewhere. Might have bin here. Might have bin takem there. Somebody might have bin pickem up, ain't it?

Him [an Aboriginal family group] bin see' em that two-feller horse. Two-feller horse feller bin see' em. Policeman bin see' em.

'Hello, what's this?'

That two-feller bin in the race, longa horse. Him catchem then, him bin gonna go that way, hill.
Might be him goin', might be hill.
Might be that way.
While him bin catchem quick-feller, that two-feller horse. Policeman bin catchem quick-feller, straightaway. Him bin catchem now, that's right.

Ride up and shootem.

They gottem a horse. That [Mounted Constable] Murray. Murray, ain't it? Oh, yeah, long bugger, long. I bin see him [when I was] little bit young feller. Havem whisker today. I bin little young feller.

Policemen, they come galloping up that way?

Yeah, right up followem that track, footwalkin' like me. They can't run away. Him bin catchem up, two-feller horse.
Two-feller horse bin stoppem up, might be him bin ride up and shootem. Might be buryem then, somebody, you know. Half-brother or even brother, or might be brother, or might be full uncle even.

Old feller going that, him cry now, old feller.
Him [?] sick, no more walk, slow.
Bin go along Mount Doreen, old feller, proper old feller. Our father, you know, father. He bin young feller, that's long feller like you, big, long.

Him bin losem [*his kin-folk*].
And woman bin go back there, olgooman [*old woman*], longa Mount Doreen.

Long time, olden time.

Me there again [*at Mount Doreen*]. I bin sit down there. I bin frighten. I bin run away. I bin just run away. *Lukbuyj! [I hid myself]*. I bin hearem 'bout. That old man bin tellem.

Nothing, you know, empty, all gone.

Two old people are spared:

Two feller, young people there, lose, and the father bin go, him cry now.
Mother and father, old fellers.
Too much.
[*The search party*] lettem go, he no shootem. Old feller, bin just lettem go. Go back long Mount Doreen.

Tape 1 Side 2

A second White man attacked: the assault on Nugget Morton

Willowra Jimmy Jungarrayi and Jampijinpa, Willowra

On the upper Lander River, Nugget Morton had taken up a makeshift station now known as 'Mud Hut'. On 26 August he left his base to visit Boomerang Hole, forty-five kilometres upriver. Here he was attacked by Warlpiri who crossed the river by night. He fought off his attackers and rode to Coniston to give the alarm. Soon the police party swung from the western area to the north, using Mud Hut as a base.

Jimmy Jungarrayi's explanation of why Morton visited Boomerang Hole (to remove his cattle so that the Warlpiri could have the water to themselves) seems a little unlikely. A more probable explanation is that he had come to check on the condition of the various mobs of cattle he had scattered about on what is now Willowra Station.

Jimmy Jungarrayi:
One man [*Morton*] bin havem, you know, our people. One man bin havem might be two, three woman, or might be two woman, or might be four woman, longa this river.
You know, our people.
And that Nugget Morton might bin think,

'I think we that one, we might robbem Aboriginal woman, or might be two, two [*ie.. Morton and his assistant had two women each*].

Nugget Morton first, they bin startem, bin startem Aborigin, our people, for that woman [*started the conflict by taking Warlpiri women*].

'All right.'

That our people bin think:

40 Part One Chapter Two

Boomerang Hole

'Oh, what about we grabbem him, *queeai [women]*. Like Nugget Morton and —— bin running with our woman — I think we'll tryem again. What about we robbem another *queeai* and *queeai* ?'

Well that thing bin come and trouble now. Other one.

All right, two two. That old people bin turn and robbem him then; Nugget Morton go and robbem our people, and that our people come, our people come to robbem our people, I mean Nugget Morton. And the Aborigin woman what they bin bringem from Gordon Down.
All right.
Well, that our people bin thinkin,

'What about we killem Nugget Morton, because they come and take our women? That [?]'

I'll tell you, I'll tell you 'bout little bit straight.
Nugget Morton gone from 'Eight Mile' *[another of Morton's camps]*.
Nugget Morton gone up, to Boomerang Hole, well there bin there lotta people there they bin livin', Aborigin people, our people — they bin relation ours.

All right, they bin goin up, look round,

'Oh lotta, big mob people here, eh?'

Yeah that people, our people.

'Yeah, all right,' that Nugget Morton said. 'You know why I comin'? I want to shift the cattle from you mob, shift back alonga station, because the Christmas comin' not long. That why I comin' — I want to shiftem all the cattle up here, out of the road for you mob, you mob want to live here longa waterhole. You know, poor fellers, you might go, you-feller perish.'

Nugget Morton, yeah.

'All right, what about you feller want to come up supper today — tonight, I mean. I give you fellers a supper.'

Okay, two, two, that Aborigin people bin coming longa him for supper. They bin givit bullock, tucker and tobacco.
All right, well that old Aborigin people said,

'Where you gonna camp?'

(You know, not English, but language, you know, because they don't have sense.)

[*Morton replied:*] 'All right, I might camp here. I shift tomorrow morning, move them cattle back. Takem back, longa river, 'nother waterhole.'

'Okay.'

'And you fellers live here, too much, you know, too much hot coming up.'

Night fell and the Warlpiri returned to the other side of the river. The plan was to attack Morton just before daybreak when there would be enough light to see, but Morton would still be sleepy.

All right, two, two, him bin layem down. Makem bed and layem down.

Well, that, all the people bin talkin',

'What [*about*] we killem that man, because that man come up and robbem with the woman all the time?'

Ask.

They bin talkin' about you know. Right, two, two.
So, about daylight, they bin thinkabout,

'Oh, before daylight, I bin murderem now.'

Aborigin people.

'All right, if him come up gun, we'll loadem up quick, we're gonna finish him.'

That old Aborigin bin comin' now, yardem up him. He trying to get hold of him.

And too late. That man bin get up now, from that bed.

Soon as him bin get up, that's the time that boomerang bin killem [*hit*] him now. Finish him.

Plenty people bin comin' up, and hurt him.
One boomerang . . . fall down.
Him bin fall down right longa his pillow. Stop that [*?*] gun.
He fall down longa him.
As soon as him fall down, that time he bin touchem that gun.
Pickem up.
That boomerang bin broke halfway, half, well still half bin stickem longa head.
Till he bin droppem.
Finish him.

Jampijinpa:
They bin want to killem him dead all right.

Jimmy Jungarrayi:
That's what they was tryin', they bin tryin', but when he grab that gun, and he shot at that two bloke, that people was scattered soon after, when they, that's the end of that two [*Aboriginal*] man, dead.

Finished with the rifle.

And they *[attackers]* scattered then. They bin want to kill that Nugget, but Nugget got two man.

Jampijinpa:
One.

Jimmy Jungarrayi:
One.

Jampijinpa:
They shot at one. Old feller.

Jimmy Jungarrayi:
And when they seen that, but they scattered then.

Jampijinpa:
Never can come back.

Jimmy Jungarrayi:
Never can come back. They all gone.

What did Nugget Morton do now?

Till him bin get up, till him bin get up, right, that Nugget Morton bin tellem him, that Aborigin woman,

'Right, you gettem horses. We're going to go back. We not musterem bullock back, we gotta go back, straight back.'

All right, that Aborigin woman bin musterem horses. They bin makem wagon plant and come back.

All right soon as the woman *[returned]*, Nugget Morton bin leavem woman — now him bin travellin' one now, *[by himself]* him bin travellin' one now. Gottem two camel and buggy, two camel bin pullem one buggy.

And *[meanwhile]* Murray bin shootem 'long, same day.

Jampijinpa:
Murray, Murray, policeman, you know. That mob bin tellem you.

Nugget Morton asks the police for help:

Jimmy Jungarrayi:
Till him *[Morton]* bin catchem up longa Coniston.

'Hey!'

Till him bin catchem up.
Well Nugget Morton bin come up, Murray bin askem,

'What wrong?'

'Ah, I got another trouble there. I bin get hurt. Over there. What about you can help me?'

'All right, we'll help you,' Murray said, 'we'll help you, we'll shootem people.'

Him bin turnem back again.

Now they all bin turn back this way now.

Tape 1 Side 2

The massacre at Tipinpa

Jampijinpa, Warlpiri, Willowra

Tipinpa (Patirlirri) lies along the route which the police party riding north from Coniston to Mud Hut would have taken. Probably this event took place after the attack on Morton.

When he visited the site, Jampijinpa identified the site where his family had camped the night before the shooting. Murray, he explained, suspected that Aborigines would be camped at the soak, and as evening fell, one of the trackers was sent forward to count the campfires and note their position. With this information Murray planned to surround the camp just before daybreak and, with Morton's help, identify the attackers at Mud Hut. At the time Jampijinpa was probably four or five years old.

The historian Dr Mervyn Hartwig has noted that Murray in his Report made no mention of having been to Tipinpa. However, Hartwig believes that there is evidence that the Report was falsified. For instance, the pastoralist Saxby, who joined the exploration party of Michael Terry in 1929, told Terry when they reached Tipinpa that Murray had been there the year before.

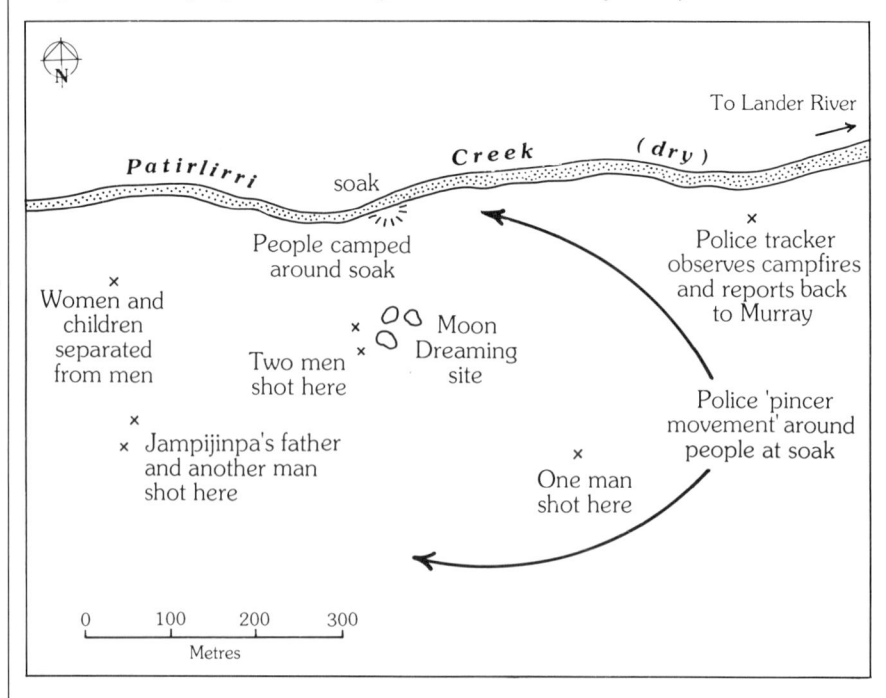

Sketch map of Tipinpa

They shot your old father?

Yeah.

What place?

Down at Tipinpa. That's this Murray bin shottit. When I was little feller.

Were you there when they shot your father?

Yeah. Little one. When I was little boy 'bout that high, I think.
I seen him. I seen him. Murray, Murray grab me then and he's hold me on the shoulder. When I was little feller. That's far, that's all I know that far.

There was big camp there, makinem, they was gettem em all the bush tucker you know, but he shot at about ten o'clock in the morning, ah, eight o'clock in the morning, shot at.
Start at eight, that way.

What happened then?

They yardem round, bringem to one mob, see, make it one heap.

And they shottit.

Two or three shotgun is goin', people is goin'.

Nugget. Whatsaname was there too, Jack Murray. They shottit, and they travellin' this way.

Water here.
But they all sittin' round here, all the old people was sleepin' here, and some people was sleepin' here,
and water there.
They was gettin' water that way,
and this way.
Well they come round with the horses this way,
and this way.

Yardem.

Jimmy Jungarrayi:
Like bullock.

Jampijinpa:
Yeah. Roundem up. Just like cattle we roundem up. And bringem one mob this way.
Just suddenly.

And just shottit there.

Did some feller try and runaway through those horses?

No, they couldn't run away.

A homeland deserted: the Coniston Massacre, 1928

Did they shoot men, or women and weeais [boys]?

Oh, no [just] man.
Woman, they just lettem go free.

But if all the people were there, and they'd got shotguns, they couldn't tell if they were hitting man or woman or what.

No, they was just draftem out.
Like cattle we draftem out cow and calf, with a calf one. But they bin just pushem out.

Push the men out?

Yeah, *weeais* and girls, and roundem all the man.
Shottem all the man.
When we draftem out cattle, we runnem cattle you know, pushem out all the bad bullock, and givem all the cows one side. That's the way they bin doing it.

Shottem.

The old woman was 'live. And kid. That's all I know that far.

Tape 1 Side 2

The police party shifts to the Hanson River

Willowra Jimmy Jungarrayi, Warlpiri, Willowra

Mud Hut

Using Mud Hut as a base, the police party scoured the Lander country, apparently seeking out all the soaks and waterholes where the Warlpiri might have been sheltering.

Perhaps it was no accident that some women and children, survivors of an earlier raid, set up a dry camp thirty kilometres from the Lander. But water was scarce and the women were forced to use Morton's Well near Mud Hut. Meanwhile Murray had taken possession of Mud Hut as a base for the second phase of the expedition. Jimmy Jungarrayi related how Murray saw the footprints around the hut and followed them up the dry creek bed until he found the

46   Part One   Chapter Two

women and children. He killed them.

Other survivors, like Tim Japangardi's family, headed into the dry country to the west and north where horses could not follow. Others went east towards the Hanson River. Here too the country was dry but there were a few waterholes which the bush people —and the police trackers — knew.

Followem this river, through there.

Now, they bin findem one old feller, two old feller I mean, two old feller, longa Dingo Hole, longa Hole. They bin finish them poor bugger.

That man [Murray] bin turn back, come back after shoot two man. They bin followem whatsaname [the Lander] now.
All the girl bin carting water from bush, longa dry camp. They bin followem and findem there longa bush. Girl and kid and all. They bin finishem again, whole lot.
Finishem, to come back again [to Mud Hut].

Having scoured the Lander country, the police party now turned eastwards towards the Hanson River.

[Nugget Morton:] 'What about we followem them people what they [those who] bin run away, after heard [of the] White man?'

Nugget Morton,

'What about we followem?'

[Murray:] 'Oh, we followem, how far we can findem. Catchem up.'

They bin followem longa sandhill country . . . right through.

I tellem might be true, you know, little bit.

They bin followem . . . right up, long Hanson Creek. But they run, and Hanson Creek that way.
Now they [police party] bin findem different, different men, you know, what they bin coming from Barrow Creek this way.
They bin findem different now, different mob. Mix up.

Tape 1 Side 2

A warning

Sandy Jungarrayi, Warlpiri, Alekarenge

Alec.

Well him bin workin Stirling Station. He bin tellem:

'Right,' Alec bin tellem. 'Oh, I think that some policeman might come and shootem all the people. You-feller have to get out. I'll clear meself.'

They bin go bush, eh? Straight mob to Barrow Creek. Travel night and day.

Why didn't they all run away when Alec says?

Some people bin way, you know, from that camp, you know . . . go cut out to huntin', get some goanna. Well that's why, that some people, old people, bin sit in a camp, like, you know, waitin' for some feller when they bin go cut out to hunting.

Too late, now, they couldn't get out. That policeman come might 'light, eh, long way, daylight, something, I don't know. Can't get out now, no more.

Tape 1 Side 2 ## The massacre at Wajinpulungk

Johnny Nelson Jupurrula, Warlpiri, Alekarenge

Johnny Nelson Jupurrula

By now the police party was amongst people who probably had not heard of the attacks on the White men. One such man was the father of Johnny Nelson Jupurrula.

This man worked on a cattle station, now abandoned, north of Alekarenge. In August or September 1928 he left the station with his family to travel to a ceremony ground on the Hanson River. There he left his family and travelled to Willowra. Perhaps in this way he missed the warnings such as the ones related above. No longer dressed in stockman's clothes, he and another man identified as 'Saturday Shannon's father' met the police party travelling in the opposite direction. Despite the fact that they were station employees, they were captured by Murray and forced at gunpoint to show the location of the ceremony ground they had recently left. It is known to Aborigines as Wajinpulungk and shown on maps as Baxters Bore.

Johnny Nelson Jupurrula described how the police party arrived at Wajinpulungk in the afternoon. Some of the Aborigines camped there escaped in the heavy timber and made their way towards Barrow Creek. Many others were captured and chained, including the guides. Two informants stated that Tracker Paddy took advantage of the fact by raping several of the captured women.

Police come along this way, come along this place here, and shootin' all the way along.

And when people bin, they bin havem, people bin makem troubles and Hanson Creek here, our mob, they don't know nothing about no troubles. They don't know!
They bin there tryin' to makem you know, corroborees, you know, something,

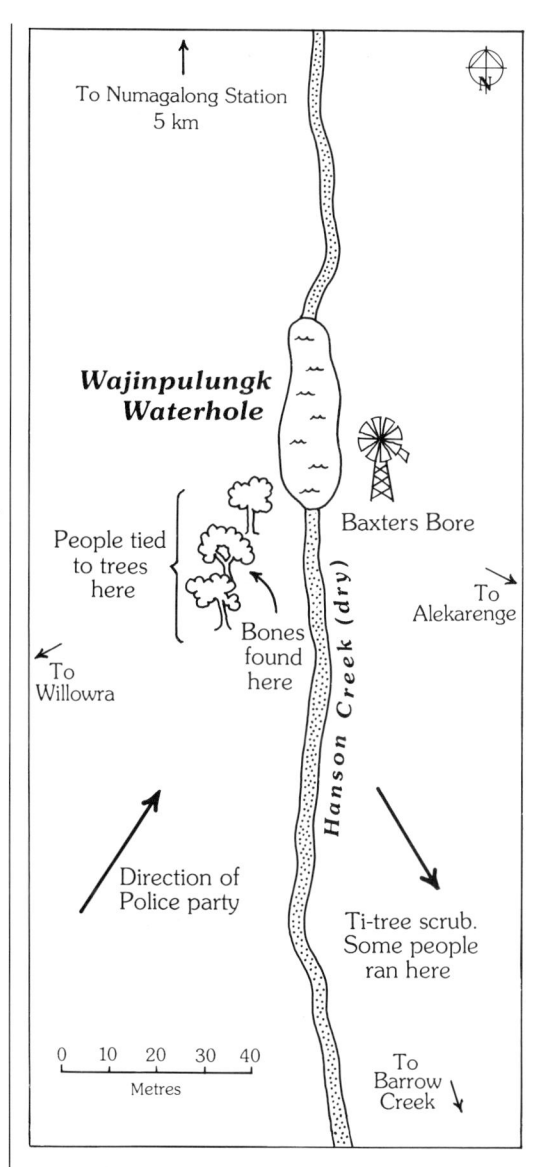

Sketch map of Wajinpulungk area

[Map shows: To Numagalong Station 5 km (north); Wajinpulungk Waterhole; Baxters Bore; People tied to trees here; Bones found here; To Willowra; Hanson Creek (dry); To Alekarenge; Direction of Police party; Ti-tree scrub. Some people ran here; To Barrow Creek; scale 0–40 Metres]

you know, sacred site, you know.
They bin havem corroboree there.
And people run away, this way, from Willowra, run into this mob here and givem trouble for this, this mob.

So the people up Lander Creek way — they ran this way, and they ran into the Hanson Creek mob?

Yeah.

Was that your father?

Yeah, my father get shot there.

And they didn't know what they were running for?

They don't know, they go away from this, used to be old station here, this side from Kurundi, they call *Miyalyiki*.

They bin go holiday, Saturday's father, Saturday Shannon's father, and my father.
They go havem holiday, poor bugger, yeah, they go on holiday longa Hanson Creek. They went there, longa Willowra, longa Hanson Creek. They don't know nothing about [Brooks or Morton].

And couple of old fellers bin there — oh, big camp in Hanson Creek. They callem, that Hanson Creek, what they call *Wajinpulungk*. Aborigin callem *Wajinpulungk*.

They bin there, big camp, living there.
And they prisonem my father.
They went tryin' to go along this, you know, what bin happen longa Hanson Creek. They want to go up there more [towards Willowra]. 'Nother side longa Willowra. They ran into police, and police grabbem, these two.
And they gaolem my father, you know, put a chain on.

Keep come up and showem this mob.

And they brought them back here?

A homeland deserted: the Coniston Massacre, 1928 49

Yeah, bring back along Hanson Creek. And pointem this fellows, you know, you know.

[Murray:] 'You can followem track too, you know. You can showem all the where soak is.'

They wanted to get your father to show them where all the soaks were, so they'd know where those people were hiding?

Yeah. And he shootem. That's the last.

Wajinpulungk

They coming there now, chasem round now, some all run away.

Right, prisonem whole lot, everyone.
Tiem up longa trees. All little boys, oh, lotta tracker, some stockmans too.

And shootem whole lot, some feller, shootem, heapem up.

Why did they tie them to the trees?

Tie' em up whole lot.
And shootem in the morning.
That's the last one they bin shoootem all along, *Wajinpulungk,* Hanson Creek. That's where my father got shot there too. And Saturday Shannon's. Everybody's.

My father used to be with the camel too, you know, carting loads, drivin' buggy and all that.

Just the men, or women too?

Oh, women and all. Not young girl, no, lettem go.

What about little fellers?

Oh, yeah, some feller. Just Saturday Shannon get a hidin' too with a nulla-nulla. Some runnin' away. Lettem go, some of them.

Did any people get away?

Some get away, yeah.

Johnny Nelson Jupurrula now describes what happened to the survivors of the massacre. His mother picked him up in a coolamon and hurried with other women to Barrow Creek Overland Telegraph Station and ration depot. Probably it was already overcrowded with refugees; the new arrivals were not allowed to remain and, with Murray still in pursuit, they at last found safety on Bushy Park Station.

Where did they run to?

They run away longa Barrow Creek way.

And my mother pick me up, like this little baby, like this one. I bin longa coolamon *[bark cradle]*. And he bringem me up longa Barrow Creek. We all run away.

Your mother took you into Barrow Creek?

Yeah. Get a ration. And *[the policeman]* Muldoon tellem 'em to get goin'. Tellem everybody,

'Keep goin'!'

Mr. Murray still busy, shootin' away.

So where did you go after you left Barrow Creek?

Oh, we goin' longa Wood Green way, and used to be old station, longa Bushy Park. Bushy Park Station.
Well there, old Jimmy, Jimmy Parker, I dunno, old feller, bin there before.

And he tellem,

'Gatherem up.'

'Oh, police come along there. Still followin' us.'

Murray's following.
And he *[Parker, the Bushy Park manager]* tellem,

'All come up, stay there!'

The station fellers tellem,

Ration Camp, Barrow Creek, 1928 (Photograph: J.W. Bleakley, National Library of Australia)

A homeland deserted: the Coniston Massacre, 1928 51

'Whatever people bin come from this way, run away from Mr Murray, when you feller bin makem trouble, still run away.'

And he puttem up paper, in a letter, you know, and we seenem [police] mob comin' then. Mr Murray come along then.
Just givem bit of paper, him and keep goin'.

So you were safe there?

We safe, we bin safe there.
Went back in, we come back in the Barrow Creek again.

Tape 1 Side 2

Months later: discovering the bodies

Charlie Jakamarra, Warlpiri, Willowra

You got another old feller, was run away from, farther on from Hanson Creek, and we run away that way, straight to Tennant Creek.

One bloke come back, trying to come up and see the people.
Well, he run into . . . people.
Like, him bin shootem round there. Make big fire, and bin come along, and see-em dead bodies now.
Just turn back, straight back.

Tape 1 Side 2

Years later: a homeland deserted

Dinny Japaljarri, Warlpiri, Yuendumu

Dinny Japaljarri

By 1930, as Dinny Japaljarri now explains, the Warlpiri and Anmatyerre people stayed in the dry country, knowing that the shooting was over but still not daring to return. At first from the western side, where the patrols seem to have been less systematic, men and women began at length to return to their country. Dinny Japaljarri describes this period, just as the drought was breaking, as a time when everyone 'get happy'.

Meanwhile the price of the mineral, wolfram had risen. At Mount Doreen, where many of the Coniston refugees had taken refuge, there was a good supply of the mineral. Many of the returning Aborigines now made up the labour force, probably by the recruiting methods he describes. The shift to the mining area in 1930–1, which could be described as the last episode in the Coniston tragedy, marked for many Aborigines the end of the hunter-gatherer nomadic life.

Big mob people we bin meetem. Yeah. Big mob. We get happy, we bin get happy for old people.

52 Part One Chapter Two

The rain came after the shooting, did it?

Yeah. Yeah. After shooting the rain coming. After that we bin go Mount Singleton. We bin big mob people, blackfeller now, big mob.

Oh, we bin get happy.

And then go that way,
stay there, big mob.
Plenty, plenty tucker, plenty goanna, green country you know. Conkerberry, plum, banana — oh, big mobs we bin havem, plenty tucker.
Rain time. Yeah. Plenty.
We get happy, old people was comin' back in — what that him bin run away. That way, Western Australia, little bit long way. From that Coniston way him bin run away, come, all brothers bin shottem here. Him bin comin' back, all bin stay there, and bush tucker.

That way we bin walk around.
Come back again.

'Oh, hey! Father! He comin' truck here. You and me might be get shot!'

We bin come, longa that Mount Doreen. Oh, truck here.

'Oh hello,'

him bin come.

'Hello.'

'Good day.'

Oh, we bin little bit frighten too. I bin *weeai* and my father bin bringit for me. He bin get the water.

Wolfram mining near Yuendumu

A homeland deserted: the Coniston Massacre, 1928

'Oh, you want to come? Good day, you want to come? Oh, I got plenty tucker.'

'All right,' I bin say. 'Father, you and me go, all along that truck. Look, finish now shooting, that people. They bin givit clothes, meat, tea, tobacco, everything.'

Oh, him bin working in the mining.

Yeah, it's right now, we bin work there. Work, work, work. Yeah, we bin work. Some people we bin work.
Then we bin grow up now.
We bin grow up, you know. Get big bird, plenty bullock, tucker, flour, tea, tea and sugar.

Oh, old people bin comin' back now. Old people bin comin' back now, comin' back. Now all bin work longa Mount Doreen.
Miner.

Tape 1 Side 2

Like bullock

Jimmy Jungarrayi, Warlpiri, Yuendumu

And they bin turnem round and shootem all.
All people, all, like bullock.
Old people bin here, this country.
All bullock, like bullock. Big mob we got it. Oh, woman . . . kid . . . man.

Too much woman.

Too much . . .

Too much man.

Too much blackfeller.

All Warlpiri, you know, all Warlpiri.

Poor bugger.

Chapter Three
Victoria River Downs, 1895–6

These stories took place in the first and most violent phase of the guerilla war.

The year was 1895, the location the rugged country of the Victoria River basin. White settlement had had a toe-hold in the country for no more than fifteen years. It was still possible that the united hostility of the Victoria River tribes might drive the Whites from the area altogether. The country was difficult for horses. Cattle strayed, were stolen or speared.

From the rocky heights of Jasper Gorge the Ngarinman, Ngaliwurru and Wardaman people looked down on the White men's donkey teams toiling far below. The wagons carried supplies to Wave Hill and Victoria River Downs Stations. In charge were two teamsters, John Mulligan and George Ligar.

There are different explanations for the attack on the wagons which followed. Old Mick Kankinang, who tells the first of the accounts, thought it was because Mulligan and Ligar had taken some Aboriginal women. The **Northern Territory Times** *thought it was 'another of those native outrages for which the Northern Territory is obtaining so unenviable a notoriety.' The diary of the Gordon Creek Police Station trooper, William Willshire, indicates that there had been trouble for several months. Two months before the attack, he wrote that Mulligan's three Aboriginal employees had run away with firearms. The Whites of Victoria River Downs Station were leaving. Watson, a pastoralist, had such a bad name that the Blacks were frightened to remain. On the day Willshire wrote this entry, only three Whites remained in the district. That night he saw a large fire, which he supposed had been lit by the runaways 'calling the wild tribes together'.*

Nine days after Mulligan's employees ran away they were found murdered by the same 'wild tribes'. Four days after that, one of Willshire's own trackers made off in the long grass. It may be that the attack on Mulligan and Ligar was part of a determined, though disunited, attempt to drive all the Whites from the district. As Little Mick Yinyuwinma relates in the second account, the revolt, if such it was, was put down savagely.

Tape 1 Side 2

The attack on Mulligan and Ligar

Big Mick Kankinang, Ngaliwuru, Yarralin

Big Mick Kankinang (Photograph: Debbie Rose, 1983)

Northern Territory Times and Gazette, May 1895.

He [*Mulligan*] bin stealem woman. He bin havem big wagon, bin workin' there, big wagon there, gottem donkey. Havem him wagon, and he bin pull up there for camp, and Crawford [*Ligar, misnamed as Crawford, an early manager of VRD*] now.

Right, they bin go down to there, and Ngaliwuru blackfeller [*were there*]; well [*the two White men*] they bin catchem two women, keepem him there, and stop there with him. They never let go.

Well, all the blackfellow bin run away, and stop, longa big hill.

'What are we going to do? What do we havem?'

Them two men bin tryin' to go down, look, and two woman — nothing. Have a talk, they got a lot of meat-feller [*cattle killers*]. They bin meetem one-feller girl, longa creek. They warnem how many fellows get shot.

'All right. Don't tell him. Stop quiet. We'll be there.'

That boy might be come down, sneak down, fixem up lotta spear and everything, puttem up right way, and sneak down, followem that little creek. Wagon bin here, and followem little creek, and some feller follow long 'nother creek here. They bin get up from here, and from here. And that two-feller man [*Mulligan and Ligar*] go havem look, him go longa side. Look... not there.

One feller gettem [*a spear*] longa bad place, Mulligan. Him buried there now, right

---

Outrage by Blacks.

TWO WHITE MEN SPEARED.

The steam launch Victoria arrived on Friday last from the Victoria River, bringing two victims of another of those native outrages for which the Territory is obtaining so unenviable a notoriety—Messrs John Mulligan and G. Ligar. Both men were suffering from severe spear wounds, sustained nearly a month previously. They were immediately conveyed to the Palmerston Hospital, where, under the care of Dr. O'Flaherty, they are making fair progress towards recovery.

The particulars of the attack, so far as we can gather, are as follows:

On the 14th May the teams engaged in carting rations from the Victoria River for the Victoria River Downs and Wave Hill stations, Mulligan (owner) in charge, assisted by Ligar and three Queensland natives, reached the camping place at Jasper Creek Gorge toward sundown and made camp. After supper Mulligan's three blackboys, accompanied by their lubras, visited a native camp on the opposite side of the creek, taking their firearms with them. As this was a customary practice on their part on falling in with native camps the incident excited no attention. About 8 o'clock, whilst Mulligan and Ligar were standing together near the wagons, they were suddenly surprised by a shower of spears. One of the spears (a murderous weapon made of the blade of a stolen sheep-shears) struck Mulligan in the thigh, whilst Ligar was wounded in the back with a stone-headed spear which penetrated the lung, and also with a glass-headed spear, entering the right side of the face and penetrating to the left cheek bone. Mulligan was the first to recover from the shock of the unlooked for attack, and succeeded in keeping the black marauders at bay with his rifle, Ligar being temporily rendered incapable of lending any assistance by the rush of blood from the frightful wound in his face. The men remained in this terrible position throughout the remainder of the night, the natives renewing the attack again and again; during the fighting the voices of Mulligan's blackboys could be distinctly heard inciting the other natives. When morning broke Mulligan assisted Ligar to the top of one of the wagons to throw down some bags of flour with which to form a barricade. Whilst Ligar was thus employed one of Mulligan's boys, known as "Major," fired at him with a rifle, showing unmistakably that the renegade Queensland boys had leagued with the local natives. From this out the attack was kept up off and on for three days, the blacks only being kept from rushing the camp by a wholesome fear of the white men's firearms. Ligar was by this time becoming very weak from loss of blood and want of rest, and Mulligan decided that they should try to make Auvergne Station, the nearest point at which assistance was to be obtained. They got safely away, and on arrival there obtained help from Bradshaw's camp. Mr. Hugh Young, Bradshaw's manager, immediately proceeded to the wagons, finding, on arrival, that M. C. Willshire, patrolling the country with two black trackers, had reached the scene of the conflict the night after Mulligan and Ligar had left. Willshire found that the blacks had plundered the wagons, scattering the goods in every direction, and carrying away all flour, sugar, tobacco, &c., but cunningly

---

56 Part One Chapter Three

Big Mick Kankinang and Daly Pulkara at the site of the attack.

there longa in Jasper Gorge.
Mr Crawford [Ligar] him bin get wounded here, somewhere, him bin run. Blackfeller bin try and want to killem, but him bin good run, that feller.
Can't catchem up.

Mulligan and Ligar, suffering many wounds, escaped to Auvergne Station three days later to tell the news of the attack. Mulligan did not recover from his wounds and died within a year.
The police and the local pastoralists, already made nervous by the numerous cattle killings and 'desertions', set out to capture the attackers. Major, believed to have been involved, was found by the police a month after the attack. The head-stockman, who had joined the police party, tried to arrest him, but his gun 'accidentally fired, killing Major'. Another alleged culprit, Harry, was arrested and jailed.

The policeman stationed at the Gordon Creek Police Station at this time was William Willshire. Since in the following story the policeman involved was identified as O'Keefe, who replaced Willshire in September 1895, this 'revenge massacre' probably took place within six months of his arrival.

Tape 1 Side 2

The massacre at Gordon Creek

Little Mick Yinyuwinma, Ngaliwuru, Yarralin

Little Mick Yinyuwinma

This account details how, presumably as part of the general punishment of the Victoria River tribes, the Pilinara people were persuaded to come to the Gordon Creek Police Station. There they were murdered.

Pilinara.

And two, two, two girl from here, [were sent] from police station. They bin go down there, askem big mob of Pilinara, up along Gorge.

[The two women said to the bush people:]
'All right, well, we bin findem good boss.
Here's the tobacco, here's the tobacco, here's the tobacco.
Here's a good boss.
We're going to go down up there. Him wantem you fellers. That's why him bin sendem me two-feller [us].
That man, him like Aborigin. Him wantem for work. Makem yard. (You know that yard we bin looking at.) Want to makem yard. He got no man to help him. Him got nothing. Him only got three tracker.'

'Righto [replied the Pilinara]. We'll takem. We'll go. As long as he's a good boss.'

Victoria River Downs, 1895–6 57

Sketch map of Gordon Creek Police Station

Well... none bin left. They all bin come in here, camp here, in this big hole.

All right, these two girl bin go ahead, tellem that policeman,

'We got all.'

'They come in?'

'Yeah. They'll be here after dinner.'

'Righto. Where's their camp?'

'Up there, longa big hole.'

'Righto.'

'Sure?'

'Yeah.'

'Good.'

Well... they bin camp here, and takem now.
Havem dinner there longa creek. And that two, them two girl, bin come back and meetem.

'Righto. Ah, you all together? Nobody left?'

'No, all here.'

'Righto. Same lot.'

'Yeah.'

The yards

'Good.'

Well they bin takem that corner there, that yard now, where that yard. They bin leavem there.

Go longa him, tellem that policeman.

'All here?'

'Yeah, all there.'

'Righto. Well, you two-feller go back and tellem that mob

58 *Part One Chapter Three*

that they can come along now, bring in.'

They come around that gully there, you know that creek, little creek. They bin come round that corner now.

Countem all the way.
Countem. He right, linem for that chain, see, because *[he had]* long chain.

'Come on, straight up here,' that policeman said,

'Come on, nothing hurt,' telembat *[told them]*,

'Righto, altogether go there, sit down, sit down there, near a tree.'

Well *[the policeman]* bin sing out all the tracker, you know. They come in from creek. Come out, and puttem chain now longa all this mob.

The bolt in the tree where the prisoners were chained.

That chain there, only hangin' up, and other chain bin round, I think, where that lump. Tree bin coverem up, you know. Him bin like that again, but chain bin round, big one.

Well him bin puttem chain now. Longa neck. Linem up.

'Righto. Gottem plenty tea, plenty tucker. Givem a feed.'

He bin givem feed for last.

Well, this two, this Aboriginal *[one of the prisoners]*, this blackfeller bin askembat *[asked]* this two-feller *[women]* gottem language:

'You two-feller mightem be pullem me-feller leg. For nothing. We might be get killed.'

Gottem language, he tellem.

'No, no. Him mightem be puttem that chain longa you-feller, quieten him. Just makem you-feller, makem little bit quiet. Like a dog. We alda *[always]* tiem up, ain't it? Makem quiet?'

This two-feller woman talk, keep goin', see?

Righto.
All right, this policeman bin tellem,

'You altogether run that way now. Line up.'

After tucker, like, afternoon.
That way sun.
Four o'clock or three o'clock.
Sing out, all this tracker mob, bin there longa creek.

Victoria River Downs, 1895–6

Fragment of water carrier at Gordon Creek Police Station

'Come on, all you trackers.'
Makem ready.

[To the prisoners:] 'Now, go on!'

Kickem in the rib, one of them.

'All start. Right! Line up!'

Tu! Tu! Tu! Tu! Tu! Tu! Tu!

Finish.

They bin gatherem up all that now.
Gottem chain.
Puttem on mob.
Takem down to that creek where you and me bin crossem.
Puttem heap there.
Chuckem big mob of wood.
All that dead one now he bin gatherem up, takem there longa that creek, little one. Cartem, we two-feller crossem today.

All right, chuckem all that there now heap,
everything, dog and all.
They burnem now. They puttem big mob of wood, there, top of him. And chuckem kerosene, strike some matches, and burnem.
Lot.

No anything left, eh.

All ashes.

Burnem finish.

End of Tape 1 Side 2

Lot.

Gordon Creek, where the bodies were burnt.

60 *Part One Chapter Three*

Not recorded on accompanying tape

Extracts from the Gordon Creek (Police Hole) Police Journal

18th March 1895
Jimmy Pompey and Dick belonging to Mulligan ran away with two Winchesters, rifles and cartridges... *[they]* will, no doubt, join the cattle killers and shoot beasts for them... Crawfords's lubras have run away... Watson has such a bad name that the blacks are frightened to remain; nearly all the whites have left, and the three remaining will leave as soon as Watson returns.

21st March 1895
There is something hanging in the atmosphere that so far I have failed to discover, perhaps it is an attack on this station or one of the other stations... to say the least of it this is a rough place with treachery all around you and when blackboys belonging to the country turn out with firearms matters are getting tropical, I must go out tomorrow and look them up and promise you I will do my duty to the very last, out in the open I am not afraid of any blackfellow with firearms, but their treachery lurks beneath so many guises such as long grass, behind rocks, in creeks and up high in gorges.

31st March 1895
N.C. *[Native Constable]* Jim got off his horse and disappeared in the grass being unable to follow him with horses.

23rd May 1895.
[Mounted Constable] Willshire and two trackers left the Boab Camp at 6.30 a.m. and at 8. a.m. we came upon the wagons at T.K. Camp *[Tom Kilfoyle camp, where Mulligan and Ligar had been attacked]*. I saw at once that they had been looted by the natives, I could see nothing of Mr Mulligan, George Ligar or anyone else belonging to the waggons and goods scattered about. The range was swarming with natives who waved their spears at us...

26th May 1895
[Willshire found a note at the wagon from Ligar stating that:] '...they were speared through their own boys betraying them and setting the wild natives upon them.'

28th May 1895
I found Watson and big party of men and blackboys had gone after the natives.

25th June 1895
M.C. Willshire on duty at station... at 5.30 p.m. 17 lubras and children hove in sight in the police paddock and called out in their own dialect, asking if they could come in. I allowed them to come on and in the background *[illegible]* and coming on from bush to bush were 13 black-fellows without spears, it was getting dark so I gave the women and children about 60 lbs *[25 kg]* of bread and meat and ordered them off, to the blackfellows. I handed out rifles to Larry and George with 6 cartridges apiece and instructed them to be on the alert, and place no trust whatever in blackfellows after the experiences we have had in the last 12 months. I questioned and cross-questioned the women on matters affecting my district, re, the late murders and they informed me that Gordon Creek Jimmy and Pompey were killed because they had in the past taken a prominent part with White-fellows in tracking up their

country-men . . . these natives know nothing whatever of the Mulligan attack as that affair belonging to the Warta-man [*Wardaman*] tribe who inhabit the eastern side of the depot gorge.

The following day a similar number of Pilinara again entered the station precincts, but Willshire refused to let them approach, and insisted on their departing 'back to the Pillienara'. Willshire left the station on 26th September 1895. The following Journal entry was made by Mounted Constable O'Keefe.

12th February 1896
At 7 a.m. a mob of blacks came to the station and promised to go and bring Mulligan's lubra in, and gave them tucker.

Chapter Four
Milingimbi, 1927

Tape 2 Side 1
Start of tape

Missionaries attacked at Milingimbi

Willi Walilepa, Galiwin'ku

Willi Wallilepa

This story concerns the attack on the Milingimbi missionaries by Aborigines in 1927.

Milingimbi is an island off the Arnhem Land Coast. A protestant mission was established in 1921, and in 1927 between one hundred and two hundred Aborigines were living there. The Reverend Harold Shepherdson, a missionary in the area for nearly fifty years, thought that the people had drifted into the mission out of curiosity or in search of a job or tobacco. They were free to leave whenever they wished, but they were strongly encouraged to stay. At Milingimbi a whip was used, and on the morning of the attack, a gun was used by the missionaries to defend themselves.

At the trial of the attackers, it was stated that 'flogging and whipping' was the cause of the incident. This agrees with the evidence of Willi Wallilepa in the following account, who states that the missionary Robertson had whipped some of the men to force them into monogamy. Robertson admitted that he had used a whip for 'annoyance of a certain nature'. An eye-witness, Andrew, told the court 'it was one moon since Mr Robertson used a stock whip. The boy was Tom . . . Tom took a lubra'.

At the time of the attack on the missionaries in 1927, Willi Wallilepa was a missionary assistant and an eye-witness to these events. He began the story at a point where Robertson sent two men to the Aboriginal camp with instructions to find out how many 'promise' wives , that is, traditional marriages arranged at birth, each of the men had. They returned with the news that Robertson would have to go to find out for himself.

All right.
This two they go down and talk to Mr Robertson, you know,

'Oh, we couldn't tell you now, Mr Robertson.
I think you go down yourself.
Too many up there now. Lot of wife for one man, lot of everything for culture for *Yolngu [Aboriginal]* people, the promise. Couldn't tell you. You go and listen yourself.'

All right, Mr Robertson go down now, come there, start now that asking now.
He got a whip, a little bit whip there.
Something. Makem frighten for the people you know, carrying that whip. Mr Robertson *[used to be a]* policeman, that minister, lay missionary.

Now all right, come on askem, start from there.
Question for the people. He said:

'Ah look here, boy! We got the idea now, for that mission come here, Milingimbi. Once you got to be cut it out that law now for the *Yolngu* people. Break the law.
We don't like you, you get married to that two double wife, here, for this island, this Milingimbi Island.
All you Aborigines cut it out!
Breakem down your culture!
You want to use one, and the Bible, law, one wife, and children.'

Now, some *Yolngu* people, Aboriginal, *[had a]* little bit knowledge. We got a good mouth. We talking about little bit English. And talking to Mr Robertson:

'Ah, Mr Robertson, you come here with too many humbug for this island.
You breakem down our culture for the *Yolngu* people, Aborigine people. We usem that wife, we married, wrong culture from our idea *[from our point of view]*, from our law, for the Aborigine people. We don't *[want]* **this** law, that just your European law.
You go away, Mr Robertson. We don't want you come and talk me any more, question asking me about, talk to me. You've got no right *[to]* talk *[about]* my wife. "How many wife you got?" Five? Six? That mine! That my business!'

[Robertson replied:] 'Now look here! I 'm going to give you whip.
Look here, boy! (Sometime he callem name.) If you don't let that woman there get married by another man . . . what about all the young people here who can marry *[i.e. what about all the young men have no-one to marry]?*'

'Shut up! Go away! You've got no business got to say!'

All right.

Mr Robertson go down now for another camp. He walking round, and come and see.

'How many wife you got there?'

He asking questions.

'How many wife you got there?'

64   Part One   Chapter Four

'Well I got ten, ten wife.'

Another one:

'I got wife there, promise and uncle, and cousin, they got to give me another [*wife each*]. Sometime, anytime, when they got a girl growing.'

'Yeah? How many? Oh, what! You're no good.
You're like a dog! Twenty silly wife!'

'Eh, you! [*replied one old man*] Shut up your mouth now. Stop the quiet.
Stop your quiet and no more asking me any more questions I got a wife here by my own business. I can havem two, or five.
And my promise girl, there, my uncle there promise, gotta give me [*a promise wife*].'

He talk like that,

'Oh, you go away now. Finish.'

Mr Robertson walking round now. Mr Robertson, he said:

'Look, I've got to whip you people now. I'm very, very cross, now I'm very sad by that business, listen, no good by you people. What about the Bible by Mr Watson [*the first Methodist missionary in the area*]?'

'You and Mr Watson now, you and mister, bin go back your home. No good hanging round the Milingimbi. You too much humbug, you playing around. Never get the . . .'

Talk to him.

'Very sad for we people, asking Christian business for wife. Want girl. You got no right got to say that.'

Other people say that.

He [*Robertson*] go go round, go like that.
Go go go go go go asking like that, Mr Robertson.

Now we bin think about now. We havem little bit meeting, committee of Aborigine people. You know:

'We got a lot of wife. I bin havem three wife myself.'

Another one:

'I got a promise. I gotta two promise from my cousin and uncle, or something.'

Another man he said:

'I don't know, but I got to changing, for myself. I got to use one,'

said,

Milingimbi, 1927 65

'I believing by the Law. But I *[also]* believing by the *[Christian]* Law by the Bible. The missionary come. Mr Watson come and say that right, I think. I can use one *[wife]*. Then we can make a lot of family. Right thing from one wife.'

'Well that's not our Law,'

another man say.

'Nother man, he said:

'Go down there, yet. No, I'm not going to leave this law.'

The meeting decided to send a message to the mainland asking for warriors to kill Robertson.

I think we people send a message now, straight to people on mainland — Gandagattji, Nangalala. We send somebody up there with a message, we send *[from]* Milingimbi.
Go down there, and tell that people, Bomodo people there:

'Aboriginal people bring back spear. We got to kill this White man, straight, Mr Robertson. Kill! Makem dead!'

Milingimbi people say.

[The mainland people] Said:

'All right. Saturday night we talk about that, for Sunday Mission, straight go there.'

Bringem down people there, enemy now, from mainland.

Well, Sunday morning, we'll have a service.

Well everybody *[at the]* service now.
Come story, talk about from Bible now, from God business . . .

Now, people they sneaking round, and ring round for we.

Got order from we people, we givem order.
We bin pushem in the people gotta kill Mr Robertson.

Well Mr Robertson bad man. He askem, but we straight by the woman belonga wife, belonga we. Humbug too much! No good! He can't listen for *[to]* we properly. *We* got to say if anything, for changing mind, weself.

We puttem head down like that,

Bob Bopani points to the mainland where the attackers came from.

'Amen.'

Something they come now, givem straight spear for Mr Robertson.
Come throw that shovel spear,
come here, throw there,
come here now.
Fall down on the table, chuck the table, and fall down here.

Half dead.

Finish, now everything blood around go.
Half dead.

Lay missionary and leader and first missionary. We kill on Milingimbi. Make you understand!

After they gettem cartridge now. Get the box cartridge. Puttem in shotgun. Fire now for the people.
And one old man, general, my father for my wife father, old man, Harry:

'We not going to fight for this man. No man is trouble come and kill this man for you, and that man they makem start dance and trouble, order, anything, temptation. What happen, I think we, no more trouble.
We don't gotta fight too much. We leave the trouble now, come down. Stop the trouble, now right out. Finish.'

Old man said.

Now, we waiting now policeman come, we send a letter, to Darwin.

All right . . .
policeman come. I bin start round on the boat, with the captain. And policeman's name Constable Mr McNab. He got to bringem down handcuff, lot of handcuff and everything. Long chain from there, that long, and up there [neck chains].

Spoil all the culture for the Aborigine people properly, that man.
He no good.
We don't likem that kind of missionary. He no good for Aborigine people. Don't like anyone like that, European talk like that, you know, minister or government or anybody.
No good.

Right:
The grave of
Harry
Makarrwala

Northern
Territory
Times and
Gazette,
4 March
1927.

SUPREME COURT

The case of the King versus Chalbar, otherwise Erranungen...
Mr Braham said that the facts were that at the Milingimbi Mission Station on 13th February while the usual church service was being held there was some confusion and the accused (Erranungen) in company with others was seen painted in some tribal fashion armed with a spear and womera. Mr Webb appeared round the corner of the building and a spear was thrown at him but did not hit him. Mr Robertson subsequently appeared and saw the accused with a spear directed and apparently ready to be hurled or aimed and he endeavoured to get some piece of wood and to approach the accused and knock the spear out of his hand. Mr Robertson retired to get some fire-arms and he came back with a rifle and fired and at the same time the accused threw a spear at him and wounded him rather seriously. The accused and the others got away. They were subsequently caught and interrogated by Mr Webb, the Superintendent...

Milingimbi, 1927 67

Tape 2 Side 1 | **Another eye-witness account**

Mick Makani, Djinang, Galiwin'ku

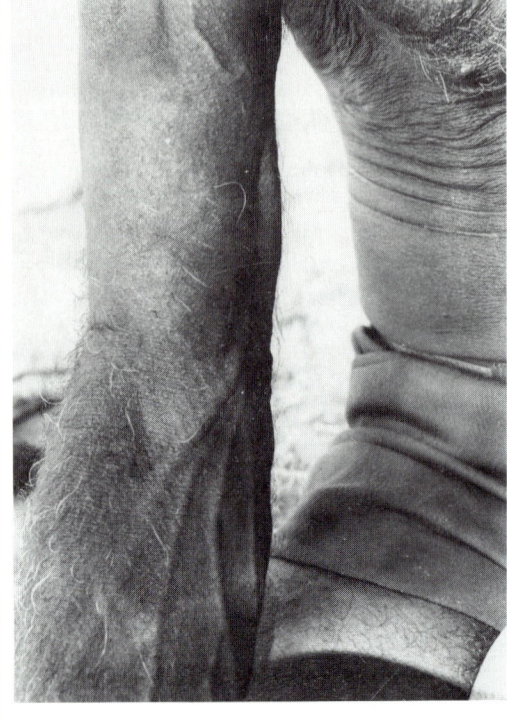

Shotgun scars on Mick Makani's arm, from wounds sustained during the attack.

Two policeman. Two policeman bin come up:

'Oh, what you fellers do? What happen?'

'Ah, very bad man, *Balanda [White man]*, Robertson, and we killem him.
We no dog, we no anything bad, anything, or work, anything. We man. We bin do. We bin do. We bin killem, we bin killem. Because you *Balanda* no good. You silly head you. Bad man you. After we, and we killem you.
Like that.
You understand it?

Mick Makani was one of the three attackers and in 1977 was the sole survivor. He was sentenced to one year's imprisonment in Fanny Bay Gaol.

Tape 2 Side 1 | **Epilogue: the people come quiet now**

Maudie Munguj and Jess Roberts Garalnganjag, Mangarayi, Jilkminggan

Jess Roberts Garalnganjag:
Then people come quiet now from after that feller bin get shot now.
They all come quiet all the way, now, now White man bin settle down blackfeller now. Blackfeller bin just settle down too now.
Now no more run away now.

Maudie Munguj:
No more run away now. No more fight.

Jess Roberts Garanganjag:
Yeah, blackfeller bin tellem him *[a station Aboriginal told the bush people]*.

Maudie Munguj:
'Ah no whitefeller, no whitefeller banging that mob.'

Jess Roberts Garalnganjag:
Yeah. Blackfeller bin tellem him. Him bin no more runaway now.

Maudie Munguj:
Yuwayi *[yes]*.

Jess Roberts Garalnganjag:
Might as well him bin just give up.

Maudie Munguj:
Yuwayi.

Jess Roberts Garalnganjag:
You know, settle down, now. And we might as well sit down.

That war finish then?

Yeah.

No more shooting?

No, finish.

No more spearing?

Nothing, now.
Nothing now.

That was when they bin havem that *[Elsey]* station.

Part Two

Living with Whites

Chapter One
Coming in

What happened to the survivors of the massacres at Mirki, Coniston and Bowgan? What of those men who from the safety of the hills waved their spears at the policeman Willshire as he investigated the overturned wagons in Jasper Gorge. Did they die in the bush of old age? Did they join the stations, and if so, did they go voluntarily or were they compelled?

The anthropologist W.E.H. Stanner thought that some Daly River people had 'come in' because they wanted tobacco and tea: 'They say that their appetites for tobacco and, to a lesser extent, tea, became so intense that neither man nor woman could bear to be without . . . Individuals, families and parties of friends simply went away to places where the avidly desired things could be obtained'. The story of Engineer Jack Japaljarri confirms that a good many of his Warrmarla clan walked from their homeland to ask for tobacco at Wave Hill station in 1928, then could not return because they heard of the Coniston shootings.

The historian Annette Hamilton argued that the bush people came in also for food. Aborigines had always chosen the most easily available food sources, so they 'moved to the Whites, not in order to take part in White society, not to experience social change, but in order to eat the food'! Spider Brennan, in an extract below, confirms this view:

'Because [in the] bush sometimes I gettem [no] breakfast, sometimes three days no tucker. That the way I bin thinking, "Oh, I have to go back again Maranboy". Every day that breakfast tucker, every day dinner time tucker. We bin stay there all the day.'

The historian Henry Reynolds believed that people were also driven into the stations by the fear of violence. 'The decision to come in', he wrote, 'was essentially political in nature, a rational choice from among a rapidly dwindling set of options.' In addition, changes in the ecology caused by cattle made it increasingly difficult to maintain an existence wholly based on hunter-gathering.

There are examples also of station Aboriginals persuading bush people to join the stations, and of Chinese and Aborigines apparently living together for mutual convenience. A working relationship was often set up with the *stations, though frequently without the consent of the station lessees, in which bush people came in at night for supplies and to renew relationships. In Arnhem Land, where there was less to fear from pastoralists, mission stations became trading posts. It is clear from the following stories that many bush people never 'came in' at all, or remained out until their health gave way in old age.*

Tape 2 Side 1

Making a choice at the Elsey

Jess Roberts Garalnganjag, Mangarayi, Elsey Station

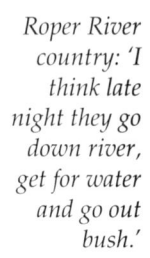

Roper River country: 'I think late night they go down river, get for water and go out bush.'

In the following three stories violence, or the threat of violence, was the chief lever to move the bush people into the station communities. In the first two, the 'negotiations' were carried by an Aboriginal intermediary, and in the third by a White.

Wild times people, I think people bin run away all the time.

Just for makem, you know, makem bit quiet, and they makem, but no more real shoot. Some people they shoot properly, but some people never shoot us. Just frighten people, I think.

And they used to come all the way, you know, followem big jungle.
They went out, they live in Warlock [*the original Elsey Station*].
You got all the way long big jungle, all the way right down, you know.

They used to live like that all the way along. Come out up here — they never go to [*the Roper*] River, they goin' bush till late afternoon. I think late night they go down to river, get for water and go out bush. Sleep in 'nother dry place.

Keep going like that through jungle, still in jungle.
They don't care [*weren't afraid*] in jungle, they couldn't care, you know, they

74   Part Two   Chapter One

just go anywhere up there. And in the night time, bush blackfellers [come out] when my father was alive, because [White] man bin go through that place.

And one old man, he's belong to my mother, his grandfather,
well he was used to White people, and he came all the way along track.
Quiet them people travelling all the way along from Maranboy way, coming up this way to Mangarayi peoples.
Quietenem Mangarayi people.
Yeah.
They used to come down and tell the people up this way, now, to Mangarayi, allabout story, you know, all White people, yeah.

Did he tell the Mangarayi people about tobacco?

Yes, for tobacco, for sugar, for tea leaf, for flour, I think.
Yes, and he used to tell them:

'You want to know these White people come along you and me place. You don't want to run away. When you run away White people shootem you.'

Used to say all that story.
Used to work, you know, help White people, and he used to tellem White people not go, you know:

'Don't hustlem much to that people. You make more wild. If you can stand by and I'll go and talk to them, I go and see if that people [will come to the station].'

See, might be late time, he used to go and see a lot of track, and he used to tell the White people,

'Stay here, I'll go look around myself.'

And he used to leave it him horse, and just walk in wood.

'Don't run away.' [said the 'go-between' to the bush people]

They used to askem that old man,

'You must be got White people in your back?'

And he used to say:

'No, White people [are] right away. Long way. Don't fight them White people. Come for give you something, good one.
If you can know, you're going to learn and know White people, and you want to know what food you can eat.'

Used to tellem, and bringem out them flour, you know, damper, like that, and show them:

'You're not going to usem that one for your painting. You usem that one for your eating tucker. He's same like bush rice, yeah, lily seed, and when you grind him and make a damper, well, that one him same.'

Coming in 75

Tape 2 Side 1

He got half our boy belong to us now

Powder O'Keefe, Kurdanji, Brunette Downs

'Alexandria Downs Station Blacks NT, 1924' [Original caption] (Photograph: L.Jones National Library of Australia)

'Oh, that man going to come and shoot us now. Shoot the lot.'

They getting up spear now. They going to throw a spear now. Whitefeller, whitefeller got to pull a gun.

All the old people get up now, got mob of spear. Get mob of spear now, ready for this whitefeller come along. Got a ammunition to shoot him.
Get up now, all come up.

'Want to spear him now. Now you hurry up! Get that spear! He's coming close!' he said.

All rushing then:

'You run up quick now. All lot stand up and spear him.'

Might be shot the one, you know. That his grandfather, he get shot and old feller fall down.

He put a spear on him, 'nother boy. He got the whitefeller back, in there somewhere. Wounded him. Go on, might be die.

'He got him. You got him!'

he said.

'Yeah, I got him!'

So he talking to 'nother old feller,

'He's got him with a spear,' he said. 'We'll have to run away. Get away now.

76 Part Two Chapter One

He got a lot of gun. He got too many, too many men coming up. Galloping, want to shoot us. We'll have to go.'

They speared him and they bin run away down there then, get in a big hole there.
Right down to the ground.

Big cave there.
They shottem there, whole lot of them there. All died there. You can see bone, everywhere here.

All died there.

Shottem.

[The go-between:] 'We're going down.'

Old people used to going down, get tobacco now, all that. Come in.
He tellem him that all old pensioners now:

'Ah him bin gettem, few boys now, you workem in the station now. Good man, that one, he look after boy.'

That tellem him that old people that want to go down, get it tobacco now. Bit of tucker, tea.

Tellem him with that old people:

'That's good man. He look after you and me, good feller.'

He talking to 'nother old fellers:

'We're not going to get wild, we go down and stay. He got half our boy belong to us now,'

he tellem 'nother old feller.

'We go stay long side the young boy. That *[White]* man bin get some boys belong to *[us]* working. We go down and sit down there, long side. Now we'll have a tucker then.'

[One of the bush people said:] 'We're quiet, and good man. He look afterem people.'

He talking to everyone now:

'We got to stay quiet, no more spearing Whitefellers stay quiet now. Whitefellers bin shooting him enough. We got to all quiet down.'

He talk like that, all the wild people. Used to be, early day.
We gotta camp long side the house now, camping, all the old people, wild people, coming in now.

There might be one old feller who wants to stay in the bush, though, eh?

He don't want to come down to that station, he don't want tea and sugar, he want to eat sugarbag, tucker, he talking.
They're not going to come down longa station. Some old girl going to stay with pensioners, they frighten.
Die longa bush. They don't know tea and sugar. He want to stay in the bush, eat the sugarbag, kangaroo, eat bush tucker.

Does he ever come in, that old man, or does he always stay out?

No, he always stay.
He eatin' sugarbag. No, never come in.
They was died in the bush too.

Tape 2 Side 1

I want the boys for the school

Clancy Warrawilya, Wanindilyakwa, Umbakumba

Clancy Warrawilya

The name of the White man in this extract has been omitted.

First time, like you know, old people, old people didn't know the Europeans see. And then they used to be frightened about like you know, seeing the Europeans. Well same with us.
But, like, one day then few went out and look for the people, hunt around for the people.
Not really hunt for the grown up, but he hunt for the kids, to bring the kids to school.
And he went all around, foot walk, until he find, like you know, the man with a family. Then he ask to get the boys or girls.

When your family came in [to Umbakumba], *where did your mother and father sit down?*

The other side.

Over there? Why did they come in, do you reckon?

My father didn't like, didn't like to stay in the bush without me, see, then they have to stay up closer.
Well, that's what he done, like you know. Bring all the kids in and he teach, like, the boys, how to speak English.
And he takem two or three boys with him again, and look for, he had a lot of people again in the bush.
They went in, and they find maybe two or three men with their family, and the — — used to stand, and the boys used to talk to the old people.
And they ask what:

78 *Part Two   Chapter One*

'This is the way —— want.'

And the boy told old people, and maybe old people scratch their head:

'I couldn't send my boys [the children],'

he said to those two boys.

And they tell ——, and still —— tell those two boys:

'Tell them I want the boys for the school. But I will pay them the tobacco.'

And maybe later on then they decided:

'All right, take the bigger boys and the bigger girls but don't take the little one. I keep the little one for a while.'

They said. And then they take the bigger one and they leave the smallest one.

Did he pay the tobacco on the spot?

Yeah. He had the bag. Like you know, he had the bag, he had two guns on his side, and he had one big rifle on his hand.

Do you think he would have shot them?

No, no, no, no.

But those old fellers thought he might have?

Like, they had the spear, like the old people, like, you know, really tough, old people. They tried to, like you know hook the spear [into the woomera] and they tried to, like you know, throw it to ——. But —— used to hold his gun too. And these two boys tell old people,

'If you throw the spear, then he will use this gun.'

Are you angry with —— for bringing those children in now?

No.

You think he did the right thing?

He did the right thing I think.

Did you forget about your family?

No, well, we bit worried for few days, then later on, like you know, we have, we had a brothers or sister, in here. Then they told us, not to worry about mum and dad.

Did they come in and see you?

Yeah, they used to come and see them, like, see us.
But —— didn't use to let us go and see father in the camp.

Why?

Well, oh, otherwise like you know, maybe he send one boy, and maybe father said to the boy,

'All right, we're going to go out and run away to the bush today.'

That's why he didn't use to let the boys, the boys and the girls. He didn't use to let the girls go out and see mum and dad.

The named White man was shown a transcript of the interview in 1978 and described it as fantasy. The children, he said, were brought to him by their parents when they needed protection from troubles in the camp. Later the men came and asked that dormitories be built. At no time, he said, did he own even one revolver, only a decrepit shotgun used by the people for hunting.

Tape 2 Side 1

All right, you can stop for a couple of days

Riley Young Winpilin, Ngarinman, Yarralin

Riley Young Winpilin (Photograph: Debbie Rose, 1982)

This story concerns 'Brigalow Bill', whose murder was described on page 29. Here Riley Young Winpilin describes how Brigalow Bill attempted to persuade an Aboriginal woman to live with him.

Riley Young Winpilin stated that his father had been one of those who resisted the attractions of station life, and had remained a bushman all his life.

[The husband:] 'White man, too far you going, trying to pinchem blackfeller woman.'

That bin all early day do that. Aborigin people never do that.

I suppose he didn't really pinch *the woman because he* [Ward] *gave that feller rations like tobacco and flour. But that's still wrong, is it, to take Aboriginal woman?*

Yes, still wrong, still wrong.
Yeah, well he didn't wantem, that old feller said. He didn't want to gettem flour too. He *[the husband]* said to him:

'I don't wantem flour. I don't wantem tea. I don't wantem tobacco.
I got my own tucker. I living on my own tucker. I living for my own tobacco. Him bush tobacco. I got bush tea. I got bush tucker. I got kangaroo. I got goanna. I got fish to eat. That's all I can eat. I don't know nothing out of you mob!'

Well he *[Brigalow]* said to him,

'I can still give you, old fella,'

he said to him, Brigalow said to him:

'I can still give you, because you come in here. I still give you because I'm — you know why? — I'm short of woman. I want a woman for working here. I can still give you ration. What make you worry? All right?'

Well old feller said:

'No! I can't leave my woman here. What I got to do myself? How am I going to gettem my ration?
How many, how many year you bin travelling round this bush? How long? How long you bin longa this place?'

He said to Brigalow:

'How long you bin on this place? You should bring your White lady up here, do this sort of thing.
Me, I got nothing to do, I got nothing to do [i.e. no reason] to give my Aboriginal woman to you. That's my problem.
I got to keepem, I got to keepem.
If I go down there, if I holdem the place, if you come into my place, I wouldn't like you to give me your missus for go to me. That's not right. I might get shot.'

He said to him.

'Well,' Brigalow said. 'My problem, that. I'm managing this place. Your fault to come round this place.'

[The husband:] 'That's right! This my land!' he said to him.
'It's my land.
I bin born this place.
I bin grow up this place.
I bin get tucker longa this country. I know this bush. I know all over the place. You don't know it. You only just bin come in here yesterday! And you know about, round this part of it.
You don't know where to go. You don't know where the water, you know *this* water down here, straight down, river water, when you go in the bush, you don't know where the water, you don't know where the spring.
I know myself.
I bin born there.

'I bin grow up this place . . . You only just bin come yesterday.'

I bin grow up in the bush.
I bin learn.
I can go no feed for two, three weeks. I know where be, see?'

He said to him, Brigalow.

That Aboriginal lady, did she want to go with that White man — or want to stop with the old man?

No. She's tryin' to stop with

Coming in 81

the old man. Aboriginal lady said to him *[Brigalow]*:

'No, I got to go with this old feller.
Because this old feller bin growem up me from little feller. He bin growem up me all round the bush. I want to live with this old feller, poor bugger. I'll stay with him.'

'No, no, no,' Brigalow said. 'No, no, no. You can't make a station that way. You got to stop with me. Trying to make this place clean.
And I'll pay you. You get a lot of money from me. And tell that old feller to leave you down here. You get lot of money. Save you just walking round in the bush with the dirty clothes, dirty everything.'

'Now you,' lady said to him, 'I bin growing for year and year and year for that Riley *[her husband]*,'

she said to him,

'You can't tell me what I gotta do. I bin born for years and year longa stock camp, longa bush. You can't makem Aboriginal other way round.
This bin start off from one beginnings in time. Early days.'

She said to him. Yeah. Old Aboriginal missus said to him.

[Brigalow:] 'What you going to do now. You want to go or what?'

'No, yeah, I got to go with my old feller.'

[Brigalow:] 'Now, if I give him this ration, if I give him ration, otherwi' I'll shoot you. I'll shoot you too. Kill you two of them.'

Well, she said she'd ask that old feller.

'Well look I stop with this fellow *[Brigalow]* for while? Just for a couple of day?'

Well, old feller said:

'All right then, you can stop for a couple of days. But I don't think,' old feller said, 'I don't think Brigalow'll be alive. 'Nother few days' time, he'll be finished.'

In October 1909, Ward was killed at his hut. The body was never found, though the police officer found what appeared to have been a rough grave near the river. He concluded that the dingoes had eaten the body. **The Northern Territory Times** *stated that Ward had been murdered 'by a lubra working about the house'.*

Tape 2 Side 1 | **Plenty short tucker**
| Jampijinpa, Warlpiri, Willowra

A drop in mineral prices and demobilisation after the Second World War left a great many Aboriginal people unemployed. A concerted effort was made by the Native Affairs Branch to gather together the unemployed from towns like Alice Springs to live in new large-scale settlements. Bamyili (Barunga), Warrabri (Alekarenge) and Yuendumu were amongst those created.

Aboriginal eating accommodation, Humbert River Station

Jampijinpa explains how his friend Jim gathered some of the people living near the Granites mining settlement. They were taken to Yuendumu.

When old Jim went to Granites to get the old people, some of them were bush people, I think, and some were working for White men there?

Yeah, that's working for mining. Some people was live in the bush, and tellem all them working fellers,

'Where's them other mob living?'

'Oh, they're camping out the bush.'

'Right, what about you fellers go and pickem up. Tellem tomorrow.'

He did, too.

Abandoned settlement mess hut — men's section

Coming in 83

What story would they tellem, when they want those old people to get on the truck?

Yeah:

'We got to go back. We got a good place out there [at Yuendumu].'

'All right, we'll have plenty ration, plenty tucker, plenty meat. We don't lookabout for tucker, bush tucker, long way, knockem up self. We gotta go and have tucker.
Tea and blanket, trouser and shirt, hat.
Plenty short tucker — lollies and biscuit, cake, cool drink.'

Before that grog, before that grog.

Tape 2 Side 1 | The old people or the new

Tim Janama, Yanyuwa, Borroloola

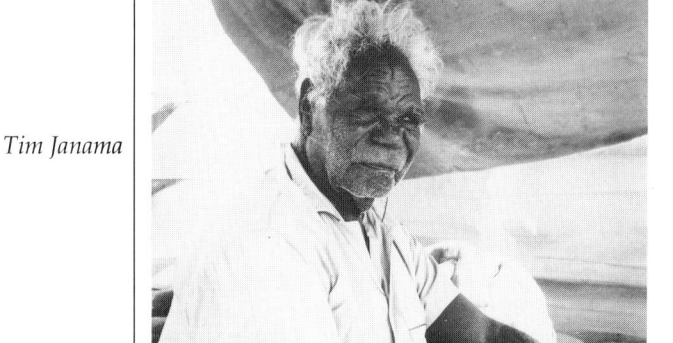

Tim Janama

This story probably took place between 1910 and 1920. Tim Janama was perhaps sixteen when a lugger skipper, Captain Luff, called at Borroloola to recruit an Aboriginal crew for a trepanging expedition. The local policeman assisted him and Tim Janama became a not unwilling member of the crew.

Some years later, when the lugger returned to Borroloola, Tim Janama was persuaded by older Aborigines that he should leave the ship: 'More better you sit down longa old men now'.

One man bin come up from Thursday Island, eh, from Thursday Island up this way.
Captain, you know, got a big boat. And him son. Captain Luff, old man, Captain Luff, too, you know Captain.
Bin come up here, and I bin young feller too, that time. I was proper young feller, no whisker.
Well, old Banjo, my brother up there, behind come up there, alonga landing.

Right he [Captain Luff] bin come up now, he bin askem policeman. Bin askem policeman you know:

'I want some boy.'

'Yeah. All right.'

That policeman called Mr Turner. Mr Turner. And Mr Macdonald. Two policeman bin here.
They come up now, bin talk to one boy. Leo, they call him Leo. Leo.

Wreck of a lugger, Milingimbi

Him bin working longa that boat, you know, him bin *Ingura [tribe]* now. Leo.

'Come up now, well, you-feller, how you bin want to come and work?'

'Yeah.'

'I want about six altogether boy. Six boy altogether.'

All young boys like you?

Mm.
All right, go now.
Roll my swag. Good, good. So bin puttem one bag big tobacco, all the way, you know, that many, six for my father and everybody. For pay, you know. Yeah, and jam too, everything, jam.

Did you want to go on the boat, or did you want to stay?

No, no, I'm ready now for going. All ready for go, you know.
Yeah. Go with, oh, big mob, big mob, and Island boy too, from Torres Strait, you know, oh, big mob bin come up too.

And you know where I bin go? I bin go longa Arnhem Land, this way, look *[pointing north]*. Big government boat.
Lugger, you know, sailing boat. Trepang *[sea-slug prized by Chinese as a delicacy]*. Yeah, trepang.
That captain, he bin go longa Darwin.
Captain, you know, my boss, go longa Darwin. Gettem findem clothes, for me fellers. Go get a clothes for everybody.

That's your pay?

That's my pay.
Oh, big mob, big mob clothes, good clothes too! Long trousers, yeah, and hat.

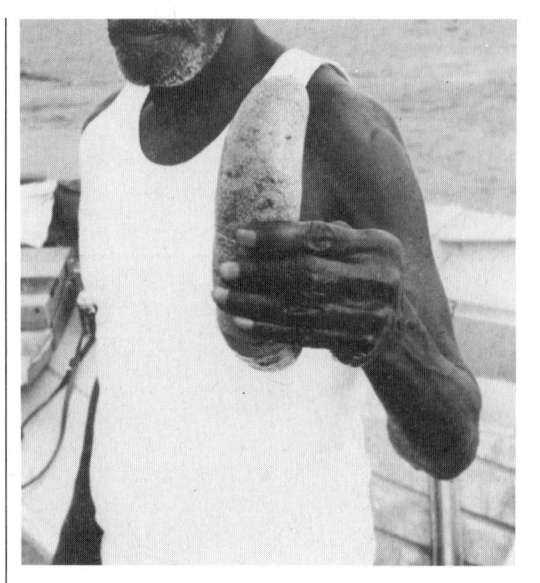

Trepang

Right, we bin work there, and that captain bin come up now, well, get there longa him, we bin get that clothes from him.

'We have clothes for you-feller, and blanket too.'

Like this time, cold weather, you know,

'We bin get blanket here for you-feller.'

By and by, I bin, well that whitefeller bin, no, that Captain Luff bin holding me properly, oh all the, all the way. That many *[years]* you know. Me and one-feller, my mate, you know, what they call Jumbo, and my brother, old Banjo and me.

'Oh, we'll have to . . .'

That 'nother mob might bin talk from here, bin come up here, get cargo here, loadem up.

[The Aboriginal cargo-carriers:] 'You feller bin oughta bin run away. Ah, poor feller, you bin oughta run away. You-feller bin away long time.'

All them blackfeller bin talking, you know, here.

'More better, you bin run away, eh? You-feller want to stop longa you-feller old man now.'

Young feller bin talk, young boy bin talk, you know:

'More better you-feller, more better you bin sit down longa old man now. You-feller better come back. You better run away.'

Yeah.

What did that captain do when you and Jumbo ran away? What did he do?

He bin sleep.

Asleep, was he? He didn't know? Was he angry when he found out?

Oh, properly angry. He bin properly asleep too.
Captain, good Captain too. He bin growem up me.
He bin puttem me captain, you know. I bin long side. I bin long side, longa him now. Captain, you know. I bin tellem all the black boy you know.
That two men bin run away now.
Run away now, come this way now, we bin gettem, we bin gettem longa night time, you know, from that Channel Island — no, from North Island, you

know. We bin jump down, at night time, you know. Oh, proper dark-feller too, too cold too.
Like this one, this bag here, I bin puttem clothes inside, my clothes you know. Tiem up.

Tape 2 Side 1

In search of tobacco

Engineer Jack Japaljarri, Warrmarla (Warlpiri), Warrabri (Alekarenge)

Engineer Jack Japaljarri

Engineer Jack Japaljarri was living with his Warrmarla Warlpiri people west of Barrow Creek. In 1928 the Warrmarla, starved of tobacco, decided to cross the borders of their traditional enemies, the Gurindji, in order to travel to Wave Hill Station. It was known that tobacco might be available there. After various adventures they arrived at the Station and were given tobacco by McCugan, the manager, in return for working on the road gang.

In the normal course of events, the Warrmarla probably would have returned to the bush within a few weeks and would afterwards have come into the Station occasionally. Shortly after their arrival, however, refugees from the Lander began to arrive with news of the Coniston shootings.

Engineer Jack Japaljarri began the story by describing how the decision was taken to cross Gurindji country. The Gurindji had to be assured that peace was intended by performing a traditional ceremomy in which the warriors of both sides laid down their arms.

This one man bin come this way, 'nother old man bin come,

'All right,'

him bin there, old man bin there,

'Oh what we, oh we got to go for tobacco now.'

We bin going to Winnecke Creek River, you know, the Winnecke Creek River. You know, this side from Hooker Creek.

We bin go big mob of soldiers, you know, soldiers, Aboriginal way. Going to Gurindji. We got to meet up the Gurindji people. They used to be, used to fight, Warlpiri and the Gurindji.

'All right, now going into Gurindji country. All right, we got to make friend now, Gurindji.'

It's my father bin make a law:

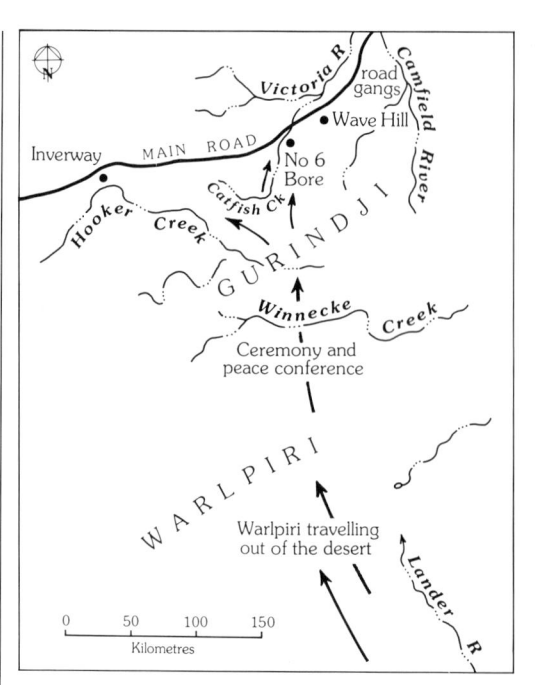

Movement of the Warlpiri and Gurindji into Wave Hill

'You can't fight.'

And my uncle:

'You can't fight. We gotta, well this time we got to makem friendly. We want to get it longa tobacco, go longa tobacco, get it tobacco.'

All right.
Right we bin go longa hill, now climb up.

And 'nother Gurindji bin sleep there, behind the hill, you know.
Big mob again, there bin big camp.
Right, they bin burnem bushfire — oh, they bin run away now. They bin findem.
All right, one bloke we bin meetem.

The preliminary meeting over, the two tribes now began a formal peace conference. First was the laying down of arms:

We all bin come, the Gurindji, Warlpiri and Gurindji mixem.
All right, we bin come out now. Marching, you know, Aboriginal way, marching.
No talkin'. Aboriginal marching first.
All right, stand up up one another, you know, to showem one another.
No, nothing.
No woomera, nothing.
All right, no trouble.
Nothing, showem that. Just the Aboriginal way, to meet up.

All right, one old man bin make a law:

'We got to get on friendly now. Doesn't matter they bin fight before.
All right, this time we'll be, we'll be friendly.'

Right first thing in the morning, first thing in the morning they bin showem down:

'Right, where you gotta go?'

Gurindji bin there.

'I'm going to Wave Hill. I'm going to get to Wave Hill.'

'All right.'

Warlpiri bin here.

88 Part Two Chapter One

'Where you fellers gotta go?'

'Go longa Inverway.' (They callem Nganguri now.)

'All right, we're going to shoot through, longa whatsaname, Wave Hill, go longa Catfish [Creek].'

Go on, finish.
Come out longa whatsaname, from station bullock too, lot of bullock, in the Catfish. Oh, just camp and live there, from Wave Hill, and from Inverway.

And the Gurindji bin travelling that side, you know,
'nother side, Warlpiri bin travelling this side.

When the Gurindji were satisfied that no mischief was intended, the Warlpiri were allowed to proceed. When they arrived they found that their reputation for fierceness had preceded them: 'Oh, the Warlpiri travelling!'.

All right, this morning we bin go travelling, gotta go longa Number Six there, Number Six Bore, bin come out longa Wave Hill.
Oh, there's a big mob of Gurindji, Mudburra and Warrmarla mix.
All bin live together:

'Oh, the Warlpiri travelling!'

and that, big mob Warlpiri travelling.

The first one we bin meet up, Wave Hill now.
All right, they bin come out Warlpiri now. Its my father bin come out.
All right. Uncle mine. Uncle bin come out, big mob everyfeller.
They bin stand up now; they got troubles before. You know what they bin kill one another. They bin stand up one another, you know, stand up one another.

All right, no trouble.
Stand up one another there you know. Big mob, you know.

'You know we can't makem fight, now. Finish.'

All right, they bin givit tobacco now.

Who gave you tobacco? The whitefeller at Wave Hill?

Whitefeller tobacco.

What was his name?

Mr McCugan. Yeah, he givit tobacco.
All the Warlpiri come now, come up.
All right, oh, bin sit down three days, sit down three days.

'All, we'll have to go back first, we'll go back first, get tobacco. We'll come back by and by.'

Big mob bin go back now, right back to longa Wave Hill. Wave Hill new station. And I bin losem father mine. We bin go back now.

Coming in 89

I bin losem my father, friendly, and old men go back.
Right, find another people, you know, crying everything. We bin sorry you know.
Right, what are we going to do? We can't go back: soon as you bin go back, we'll come back again.

All right, we go back longa Wave Hill again.
You know, bin sit down, but we got to givit job now. You-feller, Warlpiri, they go to cleanem road, you know. Yeah, just pickem up all the way rock, you know.

All right, they bin puttem three lot.
'Nother mob that way,
'Nother mob that way.
'Nother mob that way they bin puttem. 'Nother mob round station, you know.
We bin working now, working together now,
Gurindji and Warlpiri.
All right, working now right up to Christmas.

Right before Christmas we bin hearem trouble, trouble going on longa Lander. They bin startem the war *[the beginning of the Coniston massacre]*. Aborigines and whitefeller bin startem war.

End of Tape 2 Side 1

Tape 2 Side 2 Start of tape

Exchange at Groote Eylandt

Ninawunda Jerakba, Wanindilyakwa, Umbakumba

Ninawunda Jerakba

Part of the interview translated by Ivan Mamarika.

This story concerns the early years of the Anglican Emerald River Mission, established in 1924. Because the residents of the mission were brought from the Roper River district, the missionary discouraged fraternisation with Groote Eylandters. He did, however, need local produce such as turtle shell and bark for roofing. The bush people wanted food, tobacco and steel axes, and for some years a reasonably equal trading partnership flourished.

The shortage of tobacco among the Wanindilyakwa was particularly acute. Ninawunda Jerakba explained that for centuries the Macassans had brought it for trade. When they were prevented, by the new Commonwealth government, from returning to the Arnhem Land coast, the Aborigines became so desperate that they would paddle out to any passing ship to trade turtle shells or tobacco.

That Emerald River mission when those old fellers went there, to Mr Warren, they sat around outside that mission, is that right? Why did they come up to that mission?

They come for mission for tobacco. Because everybody people want tobacco. They come for mission.

90 Part Two Chapter One

Bark roof at Groote Eylandt Mission, 1928. (Photograph: State Library of South Australia)

Mr Warren, he gave you tobacco?

Yeah, plenty they givit tobacco.

Did you have to work at that mission?

Yes. We want tobacco. They want work.

What work did you have to do?

Garden work, cutting bark, bark painting or bark for roof.

How much tobacco did he give you?

[Translation:] They bin working. After when they finish, they bin get ten smoke each.
They bin work there, and when they bin finish the work they bin get ten, ten smoke each. And they bin just went back home to bush.
When they bin finish, when they bin run out of smoke, they bin came back again, gettin' smokes and tucker, like that.
Like, they bin catch any turtles, they bin go sell it to mission, they bin get smoke. Like they bin catch something, and they bin go sellem if they bin want axe, they bin just gettem, or knife, they bin just gettem.

Tape 2 Side 2

Because with his son he must come back

Johnny Nelson Jupurrula, Warlpiri, Alekarenge

This story concerns Murray Downs Station in the 1930s. By this time, most station managers had sufficient Aboriginal labour and discouraged the visits of non-working relatives. The desire to visit relatives and the desire for food are two reasons cited here for the visits of bush people, made, for obvious reasons, at night.

Coming in 91

Johnny Nelson Jupurrula begins by describing what the manager would do to bush people found on the station:

[*The station manager chased away the bush people*] Chasem out, gottem horses.

And they gonna huntem out, and [*bush people*] goin' to come sneaking in the night. Come up, get a feed.
Tea and sugar and tobacco, something, for his 'lation, you know.
Might be his son, when him working, son. Come up in the night, pickem up.

Oh, 'nother mob station used to be pretty rough.

What would he [the manager] *do if he found those relations sneaking in at night?*

Oh, he's chasem out . . . with a whip.

Would they come back again after that?

Oh, might be pickitabout, go round in bush again, come back again. Because, with his son, or uncle, something, he's gonna, must come back.
That's it.

And Fred Harris [the manager] *though, he fed all the relations?*

Oh yes, oh he feed everybody.

What if you'd run away from Murray Downs?

Oh, he's pretty cheeky. He didn't likem for cattle [*in case the bush people disturbed the cattle*]. You know cattle walk around there. Lot of cattle, might chasem out cattle. He only worry for cattle.

Tape 2 Side 2

Keep away from waterhole

Sandy Jungarrayi, Warlpiri, Willowra

Under the Aboriginal Ordinance, bush Aboriginals were allowed free use of all natural rivers and soaks, but not necessarily those bores constructed by the pastoralists.

Sandy Jungarrayi began working for the Native Affairs Branch, which he refers to as 'Welfare', in the 1940s. One of his tasks was to 'explain' to the bush people the meaning of the Ordinance. His work was reinforced by the more effective arm of the police, including Mounted Constable William Murray. Sandy Jungarrayi's account of the evictions from waterholes is followed by an extract from Murray's Station Journal describing similar activity.

We had to go and help Welfare now.
When we bin get bigger, we had to help. We had to help Welfare now.
Welfare bin chasem all over the country, you know:

'Don't come any more to station [*said Sandy Jungarrayi to the bush people*],
You know, longa station, might be some cheeky man for that station.

And don't come near here, go back.
That welfare say we got to stop one place now.
Round one side.
Don't come any more this side. No more.'

You'd go out to those old fellers, and say, 'Hey! keep away from Stirling Station!' Keep away from waterhole too? And soaks?

Yeah, keep away from waterhole. To go back and drink [*from*] one, only one bore, that's all. Don't go any bore, drinkin' waterhole.
Well, a lot of bullock runnin' waterhole, through the waterhole, and you got only drink on only one bore station.
That's all. Don't go any more.

Which bore was this one?

Any bore.
Might be station. Stirling Station might be bore, or might be Barrow Creek bore, something, government bore, you know. That's all.

'Don't go more farther because there's lotta cattle round out that there, long' every waterhole,' you know.

'Cause some station fellers goin' mustering, you know. So they keepem 'way to drink, any bore. That's it, don't get any more farther.

Bore there, bore there, bore there, bore there . . . And the old fellers could only go to that one?

That's all, they got to come here then.

Not allowed to go to that one?

No, you got to come to this bore.
And go back to the station then, see?
That's all.
When he go to hunting, when he go hunting, get kangaroo, he gotta come back to that bore. Don't eat it, come only half way, don't go more further 'nother side.
If he get one kangaroo, might be two kangaroo, well he got to come to that bore. And from bore you got to down right back [*to*] station.

That's what they bin doing before, early early day.

Not recorded on accompanying tape

Extract from Barrow Creek Police Station Journal

4th December, 1927
M.C. [*Mounted Constable*] Murray and Tracker Dan per car to Stirling Station interviewed Mr Spencer. Thence to Merino Well Cautioned Natives camped there, and ordered thence to disperse to their respective localities, returned to Stirling. Thence by horse visited Aboriginal camp and dispersed the visiting inhabitants destroyed a number of dogs, and returned to Barrow Creek per car.

Chapter Two
Learning the alien culture

This chapter describes the various ways in which Aborigines discovered some aspects of the culture of the Whites, or which they were encouraged or compelled to adopt. Some children were curious, others were removed from their parents and placed in dormitories. Children whose parents worked on stations often were initiated into stock work at seven or eight years of age.

Adults were more often drawn into White society by work and the promise of rations.

Tape 2 Side 2

Baking powder

Jerry Jangala, Warlpiri, Lajamanu

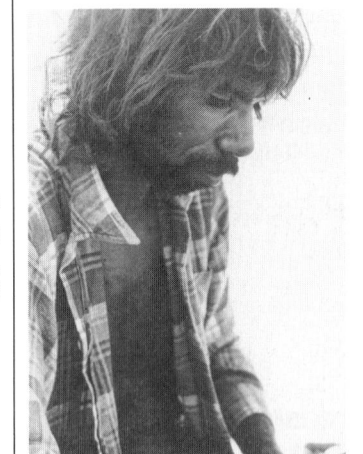

Jerry Jangala
(Photograph:
Ludo Kuipers,
1977)

Interviewed by Ludo Kuipers.

Anyhow see where that big fire, ready for lunch too.
And first time I went and watch, I didn't know what he was. Anyhow, she [*the missionary*] grabbem with the billycan, grabbem water, and pour into flour, and start mix it up. And I can watch.

'Oh, yes, he's coming, bit funny.'

You know, coming like, some sort of come, you know, like, might be rubber. And that's what I was reckon.
So...
I was watching and she make a one [damper] and just put it in the fire, and I can watch the flour.
Swelling up, you know. And I reckon, might be,

'Oh, that, that going to be bad, you know.'

*'I was watch-
ing and she
make a one
[damper]...'*

I just get up, and just move out, stand and watch, because I didn't know what was that.
And so the woman said to me,

'Why are you move away?'

and I said,

'Look at that one, he's coming out, maybe going to start you know, blow up, something like that.'

This woman turned and start breakem now, you know, breakem them johnny cake, and she give to me, half one. And I was you know, not make sure, you know, quite sure about it. I didn't make sure, really, you know.
So I got to make sure. Look.

And . . . just put it into my mouth, just a little bit, just take little bit, and start testing, you know. And she said to me:

'That's the tucker. You've got to eat that tucker.'

And then she said to me, you know with, you know, her own language.
So I was just trying it little bit by little bit, and till the next day I was, you know, getting used for using that tucker.
I was know him, now, you know.

I bin start learning.

Tape 2 Side 2

Flour, tobacco and matches

Rory Wudul Biyangunu, Garrwa, Borroloola

Roy Wudul Biyangunu spent much of his life working at Robinson River Station. Here he recalls the time, probably about 1910, when the station managers were short of labour, and needed to persuade the bush people to join them.

My father bin work longa cuttem bark.
White man, some feller makem humpy, bark humpy. No more iron [*yet*]. That old people bin work, work. White man puttem givit job:

'You go gettem bark for me.'

Learning the alien culture

Rory Wudul Biyangunu (Photograph: Ted Furbey)

Well, he bin gettem big mob longa my father, big mob people, White men working.

'Go and cuttem there.'

Well cuttem timber. Cuttem all the time timber. White man bin havem timber and dray.
All right. Some feller cuttem now, you know. Him bin feedem plenty tucker, when they work. One day they bin work, finish up.
All right:

'Well, all you boys, old men, you gotta go out bush. I'll give you bag of flour and tobacco.'

Like work, you know. You might be cuttem timber and puttem house, finish house.
Well, your boss he bin oughta say:

'All you three-feller, you got to finish work now.
I'll give you plenty tucker, plenty flour, you know, might be three drum, no, bag of flour, like people really feedem, yeah.
White people tobacco . . . you gotta learnem, you gotta learnem tobacco, anything, tell White people.
You gotta learnem White men, all the time learnem. Tobacco, smoke, matches, lightem.
You bin throw away that old thing now, that bush turn-out. Him throwem away.'

Him little bit English now longa head, longa brains, you know.

'You bin oughta have matches. Matches. Yeah. You bin oughta chuck it away that old stuff, you know, that bush one.'

Throw away all that bush stuff?

'White man bin havem timber and dray.' (Photograph: Mitchell Library, State Library of NSW)

Yuwayi.
Some people bin civilised, you know. White people, when they travellin', travel and makem quiet. Quieten him down. Some people, him run away, some feller don't likem.

They like that bush better?

Yes, but some people when they bin learn long' whitefeller, they bin learnem everything they eat. That different tobacco, matches. What they bin learn.

Tape 2 Side 2

The dormitory

Topsy Nelson Napurrula, Kaytej, Phillip Creek

Topsy Nelson Napurrula

Phillip Creek was an Anglican Mission north of Tennant Creek. It was closed during the 1950s and the people moved to Alekarenge. Topsy Nelson lived there for a time, separated from her parents, in a children's dormitory.

Here she describes how she ran away to join them after hiding in a garbage tin.

Some kids cry, might be?

I did, once.
I didn't want go.
I ran away, once. And missionary start looking for me and I was very sad for my mum and dad.
And . . . he was still carrying me and put me in, lock me in dormitory, inside. And I was crying and crying.

You couldn't stay out at night and come, visit you, visit your mother and father in the afternoon time, maybe?

Yeah, and they used to come down in the morning time, sometimes, or lunchtime when we used to be finish school, and just play around.
And they used to come in and stay, talk with us.

If your parents wanted you to go away somewhere, hunting somewhere else — they'd have to leave you behind if they wanted to go to some other part of the country, for ceremony or something? They couldn't take you with them?

No. They used to go self.
Yeah . . . For [ceremonial] business or somewhere else, hunting or campin' out for long weekend, and we used to stay one place [Phillip Creek].

Learning the alien culture

Topsy Nelson Napurrula at the site of Phillip Creek Mission, 1977

Sometimes parents was come sometime, come and see us, and we was, bit, you know, we didn't sometimes, kids, we didn't much worry about mother and father now. We used to play one place, and stay one place because we was bit used to it.

You'd forget about your mother and father?

Yeah.

So, if there's a ceremony, or business on, you couldn't go?

No.

What about during the day, Topsy? Did the mothers, the women, ever sing then so you could sit with them?

No, not in this place.
Because . . . because the missionary didn't allow much, can't see them business. The missionary was keep telling us:

'Ah, don't go to rubbish place *[i.e. the ceremonial ground]* and don't follow your mother and father. Gotta learn something. Gotta learn this way. Follow this one.'

You mean, follow Christian way?

Yeah. Christian way. Whitefeller way.

Did your mother and father, did they work around the mission? Did they, fathers, might be, do some work?

Yeah. My father used to have goats, you know, lotta goats. He used to takem

round the bush, and bringit back, puttem in yard.
And my mother, same, used to work, and sometimes, might be my mother go somewhere and get some bush food. Go out to bush.
My father was used to stop with goats.

Some kids run away from the mission?

Yeah.

Where did they run to?

Once my mother and father they went away you know. And I went to camp and I ask one of them ladies, old ladies,

'Where's my dad and mum?'

And they said to me,

'They're gone.'

I come back, to dormitory. Afternoon time I was thinking, and I couldn't stop cry. Just thinking for my mum, and cryin'.
Next day I got away.

Ran away?

Yuwayi.

Which way'd you go?

To Tennant Creek.

Did you walk?

Yeah.

Your father and mother there? Did you find them?

Yeah, yeah.

Which one did you go with?

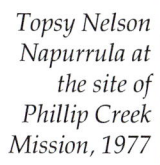

Nobody.

In the daytime, when you ran away?

In night.

Night time! By yourself!

And they was looking for me. And some other kids was telling them:

Topsy Nelson Napurrula at the site of Phillip Creek Mission, 1977

Learning the alien culture 99

'Topsy's not here. She's gone. And she went, to be with his *[her]* mother and father!'

Because my father took that other thing down to that place, to that old Station, that old Telegraph Station, he took goat there.
And that's why I couldn't stay 'ere. So I was keep thinking. And missionary was go down, and tryin' to come and bring me back.
And I run away again.

How long did it take you to walk into Tennant Creek from here? [By road 28 kilometres.]

But I didn't walk on bitumen. I walked, went straight across in the bush.

Did you know where there was water?

No.

At night I was keep walking and walking, walking, walking.
Near that Three Way I was, just have a rest there for a little while. Just listening for bird, and I was sitting in the tree.
And in the morning I was start walking, and I saw, oh, it's a bit close to me now.

That Tennant Creek?

Yuwayi.
I was walking happy way. Bit glad to see my mother and father.

Some places, they lock those dormitories at night so the kids can't get out . . .

Yes, they used to do *[that]* here.

Did you get out through the window maybe?

No. I was hiding.

I was hiding behind the kitchen in the rubbish bin.

In the rubbish bin?

Yeah. I was hiding. They was telling,

'Come on in you kids, ready for bed!'

And I was creeping along.

Tape 2 Side 2

Language

Hagar Roberts, Alawa, Hodgson Downs Station

Hagar Roberts

Hagar Roberts explains that because she was separated from her parents by missionaries who placed her in the Roper River Mission, she lost her ability to speak Alawa. The only adult Aboriginal company the children had at the mission station were two young 'mission helpers' from the neighbouring Mara tribe.

Why don't you know Alawa any more? Don't use him?

No, I don't know much. I don't know much, you see.

What language did you speak at Roper, at that mission station?

I never bin speak there, just because my father never bin against us *[never was close to us]*.
And mother, if mother teaching us, from small, but quite well. *[Usually Hagar's parents would]* Usually say that word, you see, speak lingo. But we never bin *[with]* them . . . no.

You must have seen him sometimes, that old father and mother?

Oh, some other time.

When did you see him?

Oh, every Christmas. Yeah, every Christmas. Some other time *[if]* they missing for Christmas. That's all, you see.

They come in and sit down at the mission for Christmas?

Yeah.

That's why we didn't learn much, you see.

Just learnt English from missionary?

From missionary, that's all. Missionary didn't let us go, you see. She bin learn us to speak, like, White man way. Know about a White God story, teaching us to know what to do longa White man way, that story. They didn't let us go to mother and fathers.

How did you learn how to cook, how to get sugarbag [wild honey] *and catch goanna. Somebody must have taught you how to do that, because mister missionary wouldn't?*

No, we bin have, like offsider, our colour, you see. Joshua and James. We had them two, to teaching us, how to find sugarbag, and how to cook the lily and

Learning the alien culture 101

Roper River Mission Church, 1928 (Photograph: J.W. Bleakley, National Library of Australia)

goanna and some fish. That's the way they usually teach us.

They must have known Alawa, or Mara, Nunggubuyu?

Both them. They usually say Mara, and Yukulta *[a now extinct language]*, them two.
Proper, never bin — they usually tell us *[Mara and Yukulta words]* but we never bin pick up, you see.
Tell us every time, let we know:

'You go and pick it up that something and bring it back.'

He bin chasem away out for we meet, you see, for the lingos. But we never bin speak much, you know. Hard to pick *[up]*.

Some good minds but I don't *[have]* good mind to picks up. I think Phillip and Silas Roberts, they know about much, more better than me.

But you know the missionary stories about White God?

Yeah, I know, but I got all my Bible book in there, that's the way I alda *[always]* teach all my grandchildren.
I'm Christian.
I was baptised when I was new baby born.

Did your father ever become a Christian?

My father were a Christian, my mother were a Christian.

But they knew their language, and they knew Aboriginal stories as well, didn't they? They knew two ways.

They know more better than I do, you see. They was use their own lingo, and English, you see. They was learn proper. But they never bin teach me, us, you see.
No.

They must have missed seeing their children. When they sat down by the campfire at night, they said, 'Oh, where's our children? They're back at Roper.' They must have been sad.

Yeah they always bin sad, but they never bin sad much, you see. They was forgive *[forgave]* because they bin know know missionary bin care us, look after very well.
And the Christmas, every Christmas, they was coming visit us, and go away again.
Come, and speak us. Got we own language.
But we never bin know much, you see, tell us to go everything like this, got the language. We usually ask mother and father,

'What you say — something?'

'We tell you *[in Alawa]* to go pick that tin, same as I tell you, that billycan, and the goanna, and the fish.'

I don't know much.

They'd tell you something in Alawa, and you'd say 'Hey, what do you mean, Daddy, what do you mean?'.

Yeah, that's what we usually say, asking. Asking: let we know, you see, but we never bin pick up all that language much.

When you were little did you want to go and see your mother and father?

I never bin think for my father and mother. Because I was had very nice teacher for us, to look afterem, care us.

Did you call the missionary mummy and daddy?

Yeah, we usually do that. They usually nursing us.

But they call this crow, from this Alawa . . .

Ah, let me think for that . . . ah. They call some . . .

I couldn't . . .

they call . . . ah . . . emu . . . they call it *juwijuwidi*. . . .
Yeah. That's from Alawa.
The kangaroo they call it . . . *girrimbu, girrimbu* . . .
And that *jidbirlirri*, that plain kangaroos out la *[longa]* plain, the great big one. They call it then, just think for that, they usually call it then.

And that goanna I told you for that.

And the snake they call it *yangala*, that snake, *yangala*.

Learning the alien culture 103

Tape 2 Side 2

The Big House

Leslie Wunuwugu, Alawa, Hodgson Downs Station

Leslie Wunuwugu describes how he grew up not in the station camp but in the 'Big House' (homestead) of Urapunga and St Vidgeon Stations. The manager, and in this case, the teacher, was Jimmy Gibb.

When we shift from old St Vidgeon [Station] to Urapunga, there was three of us, Peter Jackson, Tommy Gibbs and myself. We used to live in the Big House, with the old man there, and we never lived in the camp with countrymen.

Had to get up in the morning, brush our teeth, wash, before breakfast.
No wash, no breakfast.

Why was there just three of you living up in the Big House?

Well, because there was only three of us, three keeps [kept] on the place you know.
And I remember one time they came up from Roper [Mission] gonna take us down at Roper School. And he told us that he didn't want to send us there.

'You send these boys down to Roper School.'

'Oh, they're right.'

What about cooking? Did you do any of the cooking for him?

No, he had woman cook. He had a lot of womans cook too. Everybody had their meal from the house.

Did everyone come up to the house and eat dinner?

Yeah, big stock shed, you know, where everybody, stockboys and all the workin' man, you know, they could have their meal. We have our dinner in the house.

He used to watch us too. Everyone got to eat his meal. If you don't eat the meal, leave if for after. Maybe tea-time, we have the same meal.

Did he teach you, you know, how to read or write or anything?

Yeah,
he used to teach us little bit, half the time. [When there] was time, you know. Teach us to read, but we didn't bother about it. Until I went in Darwin, stop, looking back then, I reckon,

'Oh, this is what the old feller trying to teach me.'

Did you work for him during the day?

Mm, used to clean the pig yard, the goat yard, pick up rubbish round the yards.

104   Part Two   Chapter Two

Chapter Three
Living and working

Tape 2 Side 2

Do you want a job?

George Huddleston, Pine Creek

George Huddleston grew up at Delamere Station in the 1920s. As soon as he was old enough to be useful he was given a job, where, from the comparative safety of horse-tailer's assistant, he learned the complex business of cattle droving.

George Huddleston

The horse-tailer was responsible for preparing fresh horses for the stockmen, looked after the spare horses, and helped the cook.

My big brother said to me,

'Do you want a job? Just come out for tailin' horse.'

They pick me up there.

All right', I said, 'I'll try him. But I don't know how to ride a horse.'

'Oh, we teach you.'

Took me up to the drovers' camp, and old lady, and old fellow *[George Huddleston's parents]*. We walked up, and after we camped there for a while, one night, old Tom Liddy give him *[George Huddleston's father]* bag of flour, sugar, tucker, and that tea leaf, and that oldtime treacle. Black boy stuff, give him that, and old lady. We ready, packin' up, goin' to the horse now, set my mark, leaving you mother and father. And they start to cry.

'I'm right.'

'We'll look after.'

Living and working 105

'Do you want a job? Just come out for tailin' horse.' (Photograph: Australian Foreign Affairs and Trade)

Maybe brother said to mother and father,

'All right, look after.'

'Bye bye, see you. Might be big man *[next time they met]*.'

Big droving camp, oh, everywhere.

You know that Fuller, and Charlie Fuller, and old Jack Liddy — they had a big droving camp there, all mix up. We was waiting because wet was on, was waiting till the dry weather come. And all the stockman went out, branding, bring the bullock.
All drovers start to shoein' horse, ready to hit the trail.

And away we went!

Go back to the stockcamp, we had a camp out, from stock camp like that. They was branding, cuttin' the bullock out, bullock separate, cow and calf separate, bullock separate, mickeys, bull, separate, cow and calf. Right, might be, maybe 'bout five hundred, have to go longa road.

And old feller come along:

'All right, little feller, pick up all with them horse. Don't lose no horse.'

'All right boss.'

They goin'. They get up early in the morning. Oh, might about five, six. Have their lunch, they get their horse, saddlem up, tie their dinner from the pommel saddle, quartpot, hat. Go along driving along. Other big boy again, my big brother now:

'Come on, huntem along.'

We gotta go catch up the bullock, and my big brother, he know where to go pull up for camp.

Tape 2 Side 2

Teaching the pastoralist

Big Mick Kankinang, Ngarinman, Yarralin

Apart from cooking and general station work, Big Mick Kankinang was expected to teach a succession of White managers the topography of Victoria River Downs Station.

Did you use to work on the station?

We bin workin' everywhere.
We bin workin' longa cattle and I bin cookin', and I bin horsetailer.
Three job I bin work.
Well I bin workin' cooking job, that [?] one, before I get grey.
I bin cooking for one head stockman and . . . boss one, head stockman and horse tailer. That two-feller man [*two men*], and all the Aborigine people, big mob! I bin cooking for that one.
Big mob.

Make all good tucker, bakem bread, curry, puddin', everything, pudding. All that I bin cookin'.
Station tucker I bin cookin' longa them.
Smoko . . . tail wagon . . . early smoko . . . afternoon smoko . . . all the time, out longa yard, longa bush.

Whitefeller with you?

Yeah, two. One boss, one horse tailer.
Sometimes two, three White man, and all the Aborigin people. Bin working here.

Cook's wagon, Willowra Station

Oh, lotta job, oh, hard job, before.

Who were better as cattlemen, blackfellers or whitefellers?

Oh. Blackfellers are cattlemen. Really.

Why were they better?

Yeah. White man little bit him sit down longa camp all the time. White man don't know all the country, because blackfeller know.

Whitefeller get lost?

Living and working 107

*'We bin showembat ... here's the cattle country — there's that springwater country, all that. We **know.**'*

Whitefeller get lost.
He don't know spring, anything, where the cattle runnin'.
Blackfeller the **best**!
We bin showembat *[we showed]*, all the new *[White]* man come, take over, showem all the country — here's the cattle country — there's that springwater country, all that.
We **know**.
We bin showembat all that.

Can whitefellers ever get to know the country?

No, because we bin showembat.

Him knowem longa paper *[had knowledge from a map]*, now, after, and puttem down. He gottem longa paper. When new men come, well, we tellem,

'This is the place,'

this place before, showem 'nother place. Him still puttem down longa paper.

Him know then.

That's it.

But we bin working for bread and beef. We never get money then. We bin working for blanket, boot, hat, shirt and trousers, that's all. That's all we bin working for, early days.

Tape 2 Side 2

Tin mining

Spider Brennan, Ngalakan, Barunga and Maranboy

Spider Brennan

Spider Brennan worked at the Maranboy tin mine, near Katherine, before and during the Second World War. Some fifty Whites camped in and around the town working small-scale mining leases, each of whom, according to Spider Brennan, employed two or three Aborigines.

Spider Brennan described how after his first visit to Maranboy in the 1920s he returned to his parents in the bush. The rations and general activity attracted him back, until by the 1930s he was in permanent employment. His ageing parents lived at the Maranboy ration depot.

At the time of the interview, the once bustling centre of Maranboy was a forgotten and decaying ghost town gradually being enveloped by the bush.

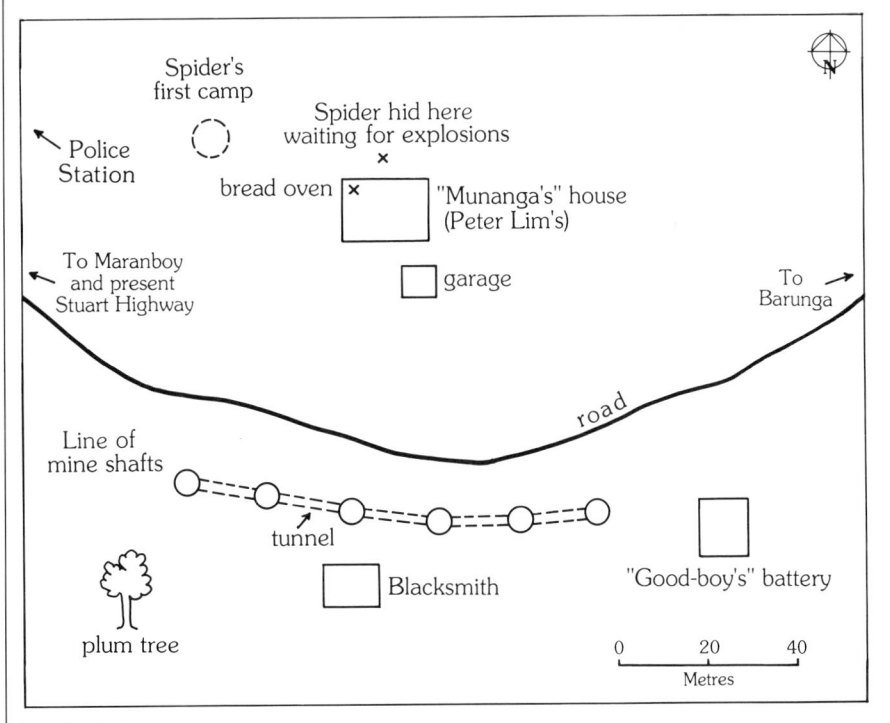

Sketch map of old Maranboy

Look that mine,
Oh I bin work little while, and go back again longa my daddy and my mother, to bush.
And we bin only sit down, might be, one year. Missing tobacco again. He *[it was]* in Maranboy.

Living and working 109

Oh, might be I go back again. Back again, yeah, Maranboy.

Because you liked it?

Yeah, oh like it, tobacco and tea, like that, you know, because bush, sometimes I get [no] breakfast, sometimes three day no tucker, in the bush, that why I bin thinking,

'Oh, I have to go back again Maranboy.'

Every day that breakfast tucker! Every day dinner time tucker.
Right, we bin stay here altogether.

Several days later, at the abandoned mine where Spider Brennan had once worked for Mr Lim:

'Ah, Spider, [said Lim] which way you work?'

'I bin finish, I bin work there longa old man,' I reckon.

'Well you come up, work longa me! That [other] man better leavem in [?]. You come and work longa me!'

Oh, me young feller. Him and me work together.
Right, we bin work together, here now, *Munanga [White man]*. And my brother, him bin come up, and I bin tellem,

'All right, you're gonna help me.'

Like that.
All right, and *Munanga* him no more bin gettem [other Aboriginal workers]. *Munanga* and me, work together, because him no want to do [everything] himself.
Gettem dynamite, straightway, everything.

Learning English:

I bin listen, but no . . . listen 'water', listen 'fire', listen 'gettem up up fire', and 'go gettem water', 'go gettem drill', 'gettem wood', 'makem fire longa blacksmith', that one, 'go gettem hammer for shovelem', 'go gettem water for drill, chuckem on there', 'makem cold, cold one, and pickem up and dry 'em up, and before [you go] takem longa claim'. That way.

That *Munanga* him bin learnem me, then I bin stop here.

The mining routine:

Somebody go down there first, and bucket him go down there, gottem winch, and I bin go down there longa ladder then, and gettem all the drill, hammer, scraper, gettem about, you know, dirt. Inside, longa wall, like I bin gettem like that, gettem like that, puttem longa little tin, puttem longa this tin. That tin now bin bringem on top, and washem,

'Oh yeah, tin.'

Spider Brennan with ore bucket, Marranboy, 1977

Keep going work, all the time.

And that one there [*pointing to a mine shaft*] big one, right up there. I used to work like that, right up here. Big plum tree here somewhere. Plum tree. I no more savvy now. But my wife him bin all day hangin' up there, look look, while him bin young girl.

Is there a tunnel between all these holes?

Yes, tunnel, for me and . . . And when I bin finish here, I bin, we bin tellem longa 'nother man, him bin name Jack Wilson, Jack Wilson. But I used to work longa Peter Lim.

And we bin findem tin over there, we bin give it him, they bin work here, work longa old claim, all the way, behind. But I bin findem first. Tin, my boss belonga me-feller, bin work, and we bin findem proper really one that way longa . . . wannim [*what name*] . . . no, Jack.
Him bin wannim, me two-feller Jack, they bin callem Jack, but we bin callem, callem, blackfeller 'Goodboy'. Well, he bin all the day like that,

'Good boy!'

Well, we bin callem 'Goodboy' then.

And we bin havem two-feller work there now, altogether.

How deep's this feller? We throw a stone down?

Chuck him . . .

And what did you use for digging, like pickaxe or something?

Got drill. No more this one [*rotating drill*]. But hand [*hammered*].

Oh, bang him. Puttem in . . .

Bang, bang, bang, bang, bang.

Puttem side, morning, I bin oughta makem three-feller hole, you know, inside.

And dinner time, makem five. That . . . puttem dynamite then and cleanem,

Living and working

put 'nother ten hole for suppertime. And for morning, puttem straight away 'nother five and five. That make ten hole. Like that. *[Ten holes made to put the charges in.]*

Twenty altogether. You drill that big hole, get the dynamite. Where do they keep the dynamite. Munanga *house?*

Yeah, *Munanga* house. And bringem here, and puttem one dynamite, cuttem up, all right, and puttem in there inside. Cap and fuse.

All right, cuttem up up. Like, no more this, really big long one, long one, up up. Makem go down, ten hole, ten fuse. Sometimes five fuse and five gelignite.

One first one, we bin lightem: one . . . two . . . three . . . four . . . five . . . six . . . seven . . . eight . . . nine . . . ten. Finish. I go up longa ladder, but long one fuse, long one.

I run this way, sometime I run this way, behind, behind that house.

Boom! We bin oughta countem. One . . . two . . . three . . . four . . . five . . . six . . . seven . . . eight . . . nine . . . ten. Finish. And go back now.
Go back. We sit down little while, you now, smoke. Cap.

Right, go down longa ladder. Look:

'Oh good tin. Tin, yes!'

Gotta little hammer. Right, go down. Gotta little hammer. Look tin.

'Oh yeah. Yeah, good tin all right. Oh, allabout tin. Oh, look at that!'

All right. Bucket! Shovel! Pick!

Righto. Gottem in inside. And shovelem up now, shovelem up.

'Don't puttem but some lump. Number one!'

All right, finish, Ah, find one now. Cleanem . . . finish.

'Oh, look at that.'

All right:

'*. . . allabout tin.*'
Spider Brennan, Marranboy, 1977

'Hoy!'

'Yes?'

'I wantem water. Sendem in water.'

112 Part Two Chapter Three

Sendem water. Gotta billycan inside, belonga drink. Or sometime water belonga drill.

'Sendem big billycan, some belonga drill too.'

'All right.'

Sendem big billycan now, big one.

The rate of pay:

Five shilling?

Five shilling . . . one week, five shilling 'nother week, next day [*week*] five shilling. That makem ten.

What about the tucker? What tucker you get?

Dish for mixing bread dough

Spider Brennan with the bread oven, Marranboy, 1977

Every week, you mean? Our tucker — half quart of flour, for weekend, and sugar and tea leaf, and tobacco, matches. Sometimes you know [*Peter Lim*] loanem shotgun, belonga kangaroo, go shootem again and come back afternoon, on Sunday. Monday morning, work.

Like that.

Saturday morning . . . longa big camp, police station, where my mother, my daddy, where they bin gettem ration. Policeman bin look afterem. Givit ration.

They were too old to work?

Yeah.

And I bin work, and bringem tucker too there. Afternoon. Sunday we leavem tucker, for daddy and mummy. And we come back longa work. All day.

You went away for weekends sometimes? Catching kangaroo?

That's right, back this way longa Elsey Station. Bamyili [*Barunga*], creek high up.

Fishing, come back. Or King River . . . walk King River, foot walk.

Monday come, and come back here Sunday, and work. But really [*long*] weekend, one month time, camp out that way, rain time, but no more cold weather, all the *Munanga* bin oughta say:

Living and working 113

'No, can't work now. More better you holiday. Good time, rain time. When rain finish you come back.'

Where do you go in wet time?

I going bit river, Bamyili high up, this way. [*We*] used to camp there, longa spring, or longa creek.

Go down this way longa King River.

When you went in the bush, did you live on bush tucker or take rations with you?

Yeah, yeah, whitefeller tucker and bush tucker.

Kangaroo, no more bullock. Sometimes I bin oughta go back, gettem beef here longa my boss.

End of Tape 2 side 2

Tape 3 Side 1
Start of tape

Droving

Kaiser Bill Jaluba, Mudburra, Katherine and Murranji track

Kaiser Bill Jaluba

Kaiser Bill Jaluba describes Matt Savage, the manager of Montejinnie Station in the 1930s:

That's all, my old boss. He grow me up. Poor feller, my old boss.

Cheeky feller, you know. Killem [*hit*] boy, little boy, brokem up, makem good you know, makem good boy. He learnem me, that whitefeller now. Mm.

Tellem me to [*do*] this way, that way. All right, I bin doem that. He bin see me [*become*] good man you know, riding horse.

'Oh, yeah, good boy!'

Never do wrong for him, no.

Matt Savage bin come when I was boy, like that. My father bin longa stock camp too, take me small one, like . . . that size, puttem on horse, takem me, tailem horse, you know, tailem that horse, [*to*] stock camp.

Droving

Every dinner time I gotta bringem back horse longa camp, like gettem horse, changem horse.

All right, takem back longa crowd [*of horses*]. Horse have a feed. Well we know, we savvy, we watchem that old people belonga me-feller, what they do. That's how we gotta do. Watchem old people.

Shoem up horse. Put a shoe on, you know, longa horse.

'Oh, that's how we gotta do.'

Well we followem that one.

What clothes did he give you?

Oh, some sort of dungaree, and mosquito net, blanket, shirt and trouser, boot, black tobacco, that's all.

He give you money, then?

No, no money that time, we bin work early days. Just for bread and beef and clothes. Shirt and trousers, boot, hat, black tobacco, that's all. No money, that's all.

Drover more better, you know. We bin oughta helpem drover. He pay me-feller. Not station. We were never paid at station. VRD *[Victoria River Downs]* manager, no.

Just shirt and trousers, boot, hat, black tobacco. That's all. No money.

Did you want money then?

No, well, we didn't know *[about it]* that time.

What was your job? You go at the front or at the back [of the mob]*?*

Back, yeah, drivem bullock.

Sometimes we gotta takem slow, you know, like this time we gotta havem rest, now. Havem quartpot, longa saddle, tucker, bit of tucker, puttem billy, quartpot. All right, boilem. All right, havem bread and beef. Damper, you know . . . some cake, when they makem cake. Sort of a cake, you know, longa bush.

You got a cook or do you cook that johnny cake yourself?

'Sometimes we gotta takem slow, you know . . .' (Photograph: Australian Foreign Affairs and Trade Department)

No, camp cook. *[We have]* Horse tailer, and camp cook. I bin oughta horse tailer.

'All right,'

[the boss] tell me,

'Wantem horse tailer?'

'No. No good.'

Horse tailer no good! You gotta go fillem up canteen, bringem back, go gettem wood, look afterem horse,

Living and working 115

hobblem up, and catch your night horses, tiem up with the halter, keepem ready, bullock get along camp. You havem supper, finish, you gotta go watch.

First watch, right up, I think about eleven, twelve, ten, half past ten.

Finish.

Callem up 'nother feller. No good!

Humbug!

Oh, big job, that, yeah.

You've still got to go on at night as well, though, eh? Like, three o'clock, 'wake up old man . . .'

Three o'clock gotta come wakem up horse tailer, wakem up horse tailer, he go musterem horse. Oh, he don't bother bringing big mob, you know, just bringem them bullock tailer horse [*the horse tailer's first task in the morning was to fetch and saddle the horses that would be used that day*].

But you got to work at night too, sometimes, eh? Watching him.

Yeah, watching, watching.

Right up, might be right up, start from eight, nine, ten, half past ten. Callem up 'nother feller, 'nother feller gotta go watchem. Bit wild one, two men watchem. When him go quiet now, well one man watchem all the way.

You sing to them?

Yeah. Sing.

What song you sing?

Oh, anything, corroboree, corroboree song . . . yeah!

Sing, finish, all right, go back sleep, callem up 'nother one, callem up 'nother one, right up, wakem up, wakem up boss one, drover boss, that and him go watchem, right up three o'clock now. He come wakem up horse tailer.

He gets up last — he makes the fire?

No, wakem up cook too. Cook that, makem tea, or sometime coffee.

At night, there's a mob sitting down there. They sit down? Still asleep, eh? And you ride round them or just sit in one place?

No, ride roundem, round and round, singing corroboree.

When him [*night*] break up, they smellem, you know, its daylight now, some bullock. Now they might wantem feed, just lettem go. They walk away now, feedin'. This one [*a stockman*] he go side [*of the mob*]. Side, tail, front.

When you're moving, how many fellows, like, five? How many in front?

Only one, side one, side one. Now might be three feller behind, just huntem up, slow.

And you go anywhere . . . old Kaiser might go at the front. Boss go in front?

No, anybody.

Where's the boss drover go?

He's come behind, sometime, and he makem all right, him blockem, makem dinner camp.

All right, makem tea. Your own quartpot, you know. Might be 'nother one stop that way,

'nother one stop that way,
'nother one stop that way.

Or might be two stop there, two there, two there, two there. Friends.

Findem quartpot, havem dinner. All right, mightem boss come,

'Right, you look afterem bullock, 'nother lot go sleep, after dinner.'

Sleeeeeep.

All right, he come wakem up.

'All right, we startem bullock now.'

I think four o'clock startem.

Humbug! Too much humbug, bullock!

At night time, like five or six o'clock, the boss says — what — 'we camp here'.

No, we gotta watchem that cook. Cook go makem camp there. Bullock going to come there for camp.

Horse tailer and cook there at that place, campin' place. Native boss go havem tea, bullock come feeding all the way, you know.

Night time, the boss says, 'Right, camp here', eh? Sit down.

All right, well him tellem that cook, you know. Him tellem cook,

'Go makem camp,'

might be five or six mile *[10 kilometres]*. He tellem horse tailer, cook.

All right, that two-feller cook and horse-tailer, they gotta come plenty time from that camp. They havem dinner, they have sleep. After dinner they shiftem camp.

That horsetailer gotta fillem up canteen, water, packem up — twelve bag, might be.

Too much.

What do you get for tucker at night? That cookie, he's cooking dinner for you?

Some damper or might be some curry . . . makem curry and damper. Havem supper.

Any smashes? Did you have a smash? They all run away?

No, sometime. Not longa me, nothing.

One time rush, you know, might be something, a night time. They just boom! Walk . . . walk . . . walk . . . walk. We hear it.

Well, somefeller gotta get up and gettem night horses *[a horse specially trained in night work, kept saddled ready for instant use]*, afterem. Manager might be come up, or 'nother boy, go there and askem,

'How're you, all right?'

Just bringem back 'long camp, puttem, roundem up and keepem.

'All right?'

'All right.'

Makem sleep, right, go back. 'Nother one mindem then.

Right, tomorrow morning, when him get up, we gotta give it kind, kindem bullock *[treat the cattle gently]*.

'All right?'

'Yeah, all right.'

Might be broken leg, or something, eh?

Yeah, havem broken leg. Well, we killem for killer *[eating]*.

Why they rush, those bullocks, at night. They get frightened?

Yeah, they gettem fright. Mook-mook *[owl]*, dingo.

So you've got to have your night horse, he's tied to a tree where you're sleeping. And boss might say, 'Hey, wake up everyone!' And what happens then?

We just go round night horses, get on. Afterem.

Oh, I bin smart feller, I couldn't sleep all the time, might be sleep, I hearem somebody sing out, I just get up. Sleep with boot. Yeah, some lazy feller him sackem, good boy him takem right up.

When did you get paid then?

Well, he paid me longa road, that drover, before I come back.

You spend money on the way back?

Yeah, I spendem longa Newcastle [*Newcastle Waters Station store*].

What did you buy?

Clothes . . . boot, hat, good hat, good boot, stock [*boots*], good trousers, stockmen trousers, coat, leather coat. Because station don't give it good clothes. Spendem all on clothes.

How much did you get for that droving trip, do you remember?

He give me . . . two hundred [*pounds — four hundred dollars*] I think. Lotta money. Cause I bin drovin' two months for him,
just helpin him.
I bin havem my own horse, station horse.
Come back, finish. We bin havem holiday then.

When we go holiday, well him givem tea, sugar, flour, baking powder, some tobacco, some matches, that's all.
Some time we go away long way, sometime we don't go. Stop home, you know, just holiday longa camp.
So him [*Savage*] might be tellem me-feller:

'If you don't like to go walkabout, you can stay there. You wantem, ration, you come up pickem up anytime, gettem some ration.'

On the Murranji Track from Top Springs to Newcastle Waters:

When you started at Montejinnie first one, could you tell me all the places you stopped at? Like, the first one would be at Top Springs, eh? Stop at Top Springs?

Yeah, we bin stop at Top Springs. No, we no bin stop at Top Springs, we bin go further down, longa . . . Armstrong [*Creek*].

Top Springs — the start of the Murranji Track

Yeah.

From there we bin go . . . not that Pussy Cat [bore] camp there. Next morning we bin go longa . . . bore. Havem dinner there.

Number Thirteen?

Number Thirteen. From Number Thirteen we bin go camp longa Yellow Waterhole, camp there.

Next morning we bin walk right up long that, 'nother bore, havem dinner there, and we bin go, dry camp, and we bin walk, come out, 'nother bore.
All right, we havem dinner there. We bin walk, from there, after dinner, camp dry camp.
Next morning, longa bore, 'nother bore, this side Murranji, they call Murranji longa bore. That one now we didn't go that place. I know that track when I bin come one time, I bin takem manager from Manbulloo. Like that he can see the country, you know.

All right, next morning we bin go to Murranji now, stop there, go lookabout goanna, killem goanna.

Top: Number Thirteen
Above: ' . . . they call Murranji longa bore.'

Bucket Creek

120   Part Two   Chapter Three

*Left:
Bullwaddy
scrub,
Murranji
Track*

*Right:
Ironwood,
Murranji
Track*

All right, we bin camp there two day. Right, we bin walk longa Bucket [*Creek*]. We didn't go that road where we bin go that way.
This way.
Black soil.
Go back like that then. We bin go longa Bucket, camp there. We bin go havem dinner half way.
Next morning, longa Newcastle.

'Next morning, longa Newcastle.'

Living and working 121

Chapter Four
The Second World War

The Second World War had a major impact on Northern Territory Aboriginal men. Though few became regular soldiers, many more were enrolled as non-combatants. Most important of the changes brought by the war were the improved living conditions. There was a standard kit issue comprising clothes, utensils, blankets, even razor blades. The rations included onions, pepper, milk and soap which were almost unheard of at the pastoral stations. Wages were set at five shillings per forty-four hour week, which, although much less than that received by White soldiers, was paid regularly and was much higher than most had previously received. Some 'Native Women Welfare Workers' were also employed. All were volunteers. The Army claimed also to have guarded the rights of Aborigines to pursue traditional life where possible.

One result of the changed conditions and a new form of corporate life were the happy memories reproduced below. Another was the perception by some that there were alternatives to the poor conditions on the pastoral stations. After the war there were increasing signs of overt challenges to White authority.

Tape 3 Side 1

Recruitment — north

Sandy August Liwiliwirri, Alawa, Hodgson Downs

Sandy August Liwiliwirri

How did you join the Army first, do you remember?

Oh, no, this one bloke just come round to Macdonald [*the Hodgson Downs Station manager*]. He only come for, you know, for Army, said, Controller, workin' for Army, you know.

'All right, I can come and work for Army,' I said.

Because no work anyway. Only young fellers, you know. I didn't care. I just went in.

And he told me up there,

'You can come down and break them horses.'

'Cause he's good man,' he said.

Tape 3 Side 1

Recruitment — south

Jampijinpa, Warlpiri, Willowra

In this extract Jampijinpa suggests that recruitment methods were not always as orthodox as the Army propaganda claimed!

Now, well some people was goin' before that, just tellem to, in the bush some people, used to get away, tellem all the people.

'All right. We gotta wait for truck. Don't you-feller runaway. We gotta wait for truck. We gotta live on the good tucker.
Well the Army's there, and if you get away, well that Army can shot you mob.'

See, we bin tellem like that:

'The Army'll go round with the war, fighting, for startin' war, but you people is goin' to come in.'

You know, tellem, got language, you know, saying:

'You peoples is coming down the camp.'

'Well, that's right, we'll be 'live.'

They did too.
See some of them old people was pass away in Yuendum' now, and some feller bin living longa bush. But they bin all come back, the Army, you know. Army bin settlem down people.
They bin right then.

'But Army was look afterem with the ration.'

Did the Army want those old fellers to be soldiers?

Yeah — no. Just for managing place, company with all the workers.

But Army was look afterem with the ration. Bread you know, biscuit, bread, flour, tinned meat.
Carton tinned meat, you know, every one of them. Old people. Well, they bin travelling longa road. Well,

chuckem all the bread and biscuit, tinned meat all the way along the road.
Yeah,
just go past, but just throwem down, to people to pick it up behind. All the kid too.
All the kid was pickin' them up too.

What for?

Because they want them to feed. They might be hungry, because, you know, Army bin worrying for people.
People was travelling the road, walking along, you know.

So they'd come along, and old fellers'd pick up those rations? But you know when you went out, first of all some Warlpiri man would go out, and say to those old people, 'Right, don't you-fellers run away, truck comin' tomorrow'. Next day, truck come. Well, could be, that when that first feller come out — he says, 'Don't you run away, truck coming . . .'

No, no, we tellem, first one go, tellem all:

'Right, we gotta go along road. Stand up there, they'll chuckem tucker for us,'

All right, old peoples gotta linem up to go along road. All right, we gotta go to road, another convoy coming tomorrow.

'See, we'll get a tucker from them.'

Old fashioned water, too
[from a drum].
Just Army truck pull over and givit drink.
Oh, might be captain, or sergeant behind, or captain, one of them.

They pull up, and some people was askem,

'What, you-feller wantem water?'

'Old fashioned water, too [from a drum].'

'Yes.'

You know, not 'yes', but yeah, just answerem with head.

All right.

'All fillem up billycan, all round.'

Fill up billycan, givit drink and tucker, bread, biscuit, bush biscuit you know, some dry biscuit before they bin fighting this war, with dry biscuit, tinned meat.
That big tinned meat, you know, big one, corn beef, that's the one.

124   Part Two   Chapter Four

The Army was feedin' peoples pretty well. Everybody was settle down then. Keep quieten down.

So when those old fellers come in, from the bush, they might be little bit frightened — you know, they're given a cup to drink, and they wouldn't know how to drinkem.

Yeah — no. They drinkem with the big billycan.

And knife and fork. They wouldn't know what knife and fork was.

Yeah. You know, somebody will showembat, to cuttem up knife and fork, see?

Well, some old people, where they bin pass away [*now dead*]. We bin always linem up, get a tucker, on the table. You know, Army tucker's good tucker, Army camps.

When they line up, they'd be frightened, eh?

No, no, no. They don't runaway. Because we know, we tellit:

'Don't you-feller get away there longa . . .'

Like, we talk language, you know.

'Don't you mob getaway, fuckin' bullet'll 'tack you.
Bullet going to stuck for you today.
He'll put a machine gun on you mob.'

You know. Frightenem, they only just learning [*from*] we.

Those old fellers, they go sneaking away at night?

No, they don't sneak away now. They know what story we tellit.

Tape 3 Side 1

Training

Tim Japangardi, Warlipri, Yuendumu

Aboriginal soldiers like Tim Japangardi probably were trained as members of the Arnhem Land Coastwatch. They formed patrols, led by White officers and staffed by Aborigines.

So you went to Darwin first and did some training there. What sort of training, do you remember?

Oh, yes, marching training, and firing training.
Target you know. That moving target, running target, everything.
Acting, you know, plane target, on a plane, shoot the high one down, or something.
Ten, you know. Or four. First. Round target.
You got to take the really, you know, sight, let you get really sight [*take careful aim*]. Take long time. Oh yeah.

And do the running, you know, running, and all kind training. Run up with the bayonet, you know, bayonet. Poke the bag, Japanee bag. Got to catch him right place.
Tough bugger them, say that. Right place here.
Got a boot, boot on it, pull the bayonet out.

We didn't play cards, we used to play two-up. Used to play two-up.
Three pennies then, we had three pennies that day. Gotta throw them up in the air. Might come, fall on the ground: then say 'two heads', and take the money there.
But two tails and one head, well, bad luck, well other people take it.

There's two men playing for it, you know, oh, lotta people really, friends and friends. [?] one another. Yeah.
We were the good time during our soldiers, and was a good fun, and everything was nice, nice and peace, you know.
Everybody was fighting, and working hard, pretty hard.

Tape 3 Side 1

A friendly sergeant

Stephen Bunbaijan, Liyagalawumirr, Galiwinku

The Army at Milingimbi, 1943 (Photograph: Australian War Memorial)

Large numbers of allied troops at the forward air base at Milingimbi led to new relations between Aborigines and Whites, unlike those experienced at pastoral stations or missions.

When I was nine, I come back to Milingimbi with my father. And I used to sit there, no school, and I started growin' up, you know, World War Two, nine, ten years old, and I used to help Marines.

What did you do for them, what did they want you to do?

126 Part Two Chapter Four

Just rakin' up and wash some dishes and clean up places.

What did they give you for this work?

No, nothing.
So Sergeant Pat think if I should be sent out, sent to Tasmania to having my schooling, but Mr Ellemor, Reverend Ellemor, said 'no'.

That's the sergeant who was there, was it? He was your friend?

Yes, I used to stay with friends.

Is he American man or Australian?

Australian, yes Tasmanian.
So he was Marine there and after that I sent out to working for Army.
They used to wash it up, polish it up, big shells. You know, used to stay in there with the one who was looking after the gun. They put me in charge to polish them, and then they, you know, they used to give me exercise for marching. I used to use the broom, you know, broom. But after that they ask the Government or that Mission again if I would be go with them to war, but they said:

'No, he's too young, too small.'

Sergeant Pat decided he would give me correspondence school from Tasmania so I used to have my schooling. Sergeant Pat used to teach me. So after that my father was very sick.
And *Bapa* 'Sheppy' *[Reverend Harold Shepherdson]* sent wireless telegram to let me know, let the soldiers know, because I used to stay with Marines, Sergeant Pat.
I was thirteen years old then, so I come back. Sergeant Pat and his big, you know, speed boat, used to pull the big barge for landing, taking the soldiers out, landing there. And they start, what Sergeant Pat think, take me and some stores to Elcho, and get timber from here. So same time decided, you know, and we heard my fathers was very sick.
What they do give me, you know, some flour, sugar, and tea and everything for my father, and Sergeant Pat think:

'If you go, and I think you'll have your schooling somewhere maybe with Mr Sheppy or Mrs Sheppy. But if you want to come back you can come back, so I'll still *[be]* looking for you, you'll be sent out to my farm in Tasmania.'

So I say,

'All right.'

They start, we start by taking me, Sergeant Pat himself, and other soldiers, some *Yolngu [Aborigines]*, lot of *Yolngu*, to Galiwinku. Sheppy was already here, and when we get here, my father's very sick, and he is happy to see me and very thankful for that soldiers, Sergeant and the others, and *Bapa* very happy and *Ngandi [Mrs Sheperdson]*.

Then *Ngandi* think, *Bapa* and *Ngandi*, whether they should, you know, because Sergeant Pat talk to them again, or something I don't know, that's what I

The Second World War 127

think happened. Well then, he start off school for me and George Turnbull, George Turnbull, we bin having together, school together. Correspondence School from South Australia.

Tape 3 Side 1

Sundays

Stephen Watson Narweya, Maung, Katherine

Stephen Watson Narweya

Sunday come, we used to have service, all round, I used to, I used to conduct.

Oh, they used to do all sorts of things, you know, play cards and all this. Wouldn't matter, we just keep on service, every now and again.

I used to sing hymns, and read some Bibles, tell them to believe God, not to give away, trust and all this, trusting. He's only the one that made us.

I used to talk to the people, we thank for the people, war people that save us, save this country. We thank Him for war people to come . . . like . . . protect, protect country. We used to pray for them.
Pray for all over the world, people, where there was war on.

Do you remember what hymns you used to sing?

Oh, yeah. 'Jesus loves me' or 'What a friend we have' and 'Stand up, stand up for . . . ' 'Onward Christian Soldiers' — good hymn:

'Onward Christian Soldiers, marching as to war,
With the cross of Jesus going on before.'

That's a good one too.

Tape 3 Side 1

Pay day

Tracker Tommy, Jingili, Elliott

They get paid, that mob?

Oh, get paid. That's the, that's the time now everybody bin, we bin look **money**. Army bin bringem back money. Now we bin showem the wages then. All the time *[for a long time]* we bin work for clothes, tobacco, bread, beef. Army come through here, and bringem money, we bin look money.

128 Part Two Chapter Four

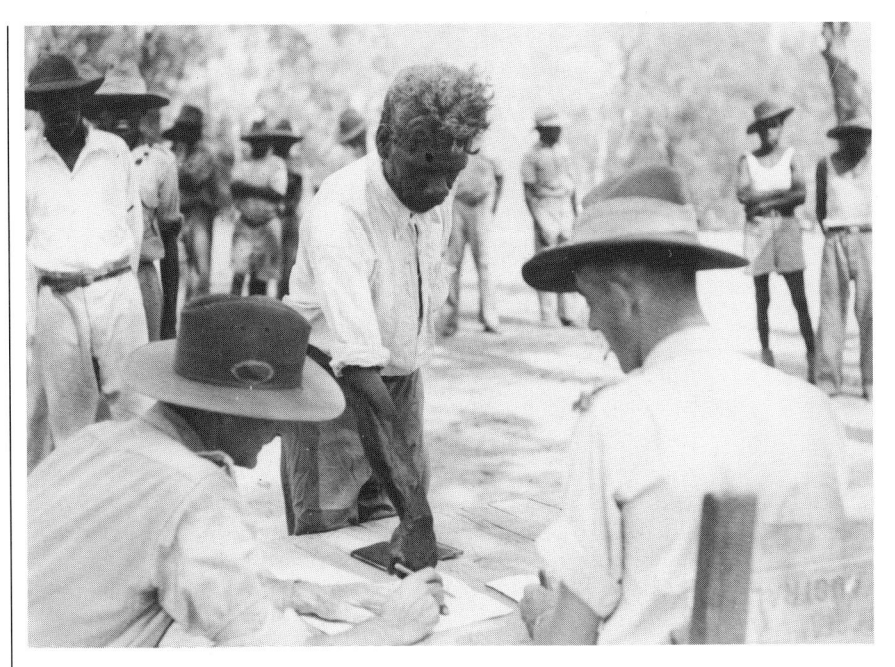

Pay day. (Photograph: Australian War Memorial)

'That's the money!'

We lookit, we look that paper:

'What's this — a paper!'

'No, that'a a note!'

Ten dollar, five dollar. We look around, we look longa we hand.

We bin only get get from whitefeller **nothing**. We bin only work, no money. Well Army bin come up, bringem money. Well, we keep that money.

Tape 3 Side 1

An air-raid at Darwin

Tim Japangardi, Warlpiri, Yuendumu

Were you up in Darwin when that bombing came?

Yeah, oh yeah.
Oh goodness, that was big rippin' that day. Bomb lot of boats' stuff, you know, boats and cities and all the buildings. That was, oh, on about, oh goodness, for two months you know.
Everybody went out, leave the city, Darwin city, you know, camp out long way. And big bushfire was on, big bushfire was on, petrol was all bombed out, oil, machine guns, everything got smash, transport, you know, convoy, train.

Did you see those Japanese planes?

Oh yeah. Oh yeah. Yeah. Yeah.

They come pretty low too.
They got really fast plane.

Oh yeah. They come right over to Larrimah, you know, with a plane and bomb platform, train platform. Oh was really bad and everybody get hurt in Darwin. All those Darwin people.

Did you see the bombs coming out of those aeroplanes?

Oh, yeah, some of them, they went up on the sky. Half way — they blow up. Some of them was went off, big one, and small one. Cause some of them never go off. And some of them went off half way. Oh that was, you know, bad, that day.

Where were you then? Were you watching from some air-raid shelter, or trench?

Oh, trench from Ten-Mile, long Darwin, you know they used, Bagot now they callit.
You know you can see machine gun sitting on the side. Lotta holes on the side, that bitumen, this side, I think it's all gone now I s'pose. You can see only a little bit machine gun, then after they got all bombed out.

Tape 3 Side 1

An air-raid at Milingimbi

Eva Number One, Djambarrpuyngu, Milingimbi

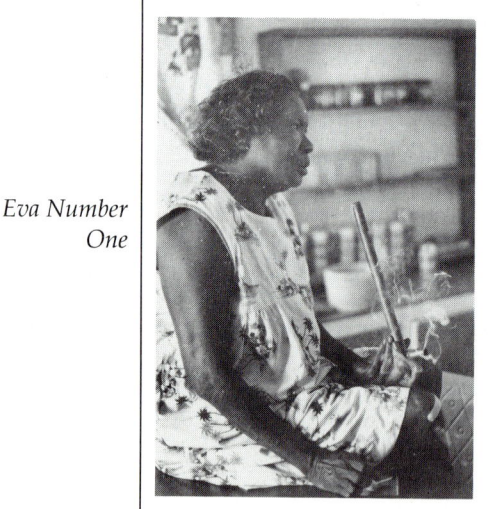

Eva Number One

Can you tell me the story of what happened on that Sunday?

I'm going to tell you a story from Japanee.

They bin coming enemy here, Milingimbi. And all this man and girls, woman, in the church, morning, 'bout the time, eight o'clock, yeah.
And . . . all the missionaries in there, in the church, three, I think, three missionaries. One English and one man from Fiji, and one man from Tonga. In the church, Fiji man [*missionary*] he say,

'I just going to finish church, and all you going to take food in the store and going away in the bush, because nearly coming now, Japanese.'

Yeah.
And all ladies and man and boys and girls in the store, and pick up all the food, take it away in the bush.
Yeah, they bin coming now, no ready yet for dinner, no cook. But they bin coming:

'Hurry up!'

130   Part Two   Chapter Four

What were you doing when they come?

Nearly walk, yeah. Some people they bin walk, behind one. Some people first time they bin going there, like, rest in the tree. And some people they bin going, like, behind.

'They bin coming now, plane, yeah. Oh yeah, Japanese coming now, comin'.'

Yeah, they bin reckon:

'Oh Japanese coming now. Come on, all you mob. Come on, run away from mango tree now, yeah.
They bin coming, shooting me.'

Yeah.

Where did you go? Did you climb a tree, or into a hole, or into the trench, or what?

In the middle. In the tree, yeah, big one mango tree same like this, see. They bin going inside, and sit here, taking up baby and little girl and little boy:

'Come on, sit here,'

mother and father, like, talk, for children, yeah,

'Mummy, mummy!'

'Oh, don't cry, don't cry.'

Mummy and father, like that.

They bin bombing now.

After that they bin finish, one, they bin accident finish, one man.
Yeah,
and they bin coming and tell missionaries. That body they bin pickem up. They bin taking away in the funeral, yeah.
Some people they no bin canoe, they bin stay here, in the bush. But some people, they, like, they bin havem canoe, they bin going away. Other side, mainland, yeah. That's really frighten, yeah. Because they bin coming first time, yeah.
And . . . old people they bin coming on the mainland, they bin camping there.

Top: Aircraft wreck, Milingimbi

Bottom: Aircraft control panel

The Second World War 131

They bin coming more planes again, coming back and bombing, large one, like, yeah.
Oh, everything they bin burn, houses, petrol.

They bin no good place here, yeah. But one week more they, Milingimbi now, in the bush, one week wait, they bin call . . . Air Force, yeah, like captain, eh, yeah. They bin call, tell missionary. Oh, all people coming back now, because gone Japanee, all finish now. They bin fighting long way now.

Street sign, Milingimbi

Tape 3 Side 1

Taking prisoners

Jimmy Jungarrayi, Warlpiri, Yuendumu

Policeman,

'Hello, Japanee there!'

I bin looking at, cunnin' bugger. Him bin two, bin out looking, bin looking at.

'Japanee there!'

We puttem in the handcuff, tiem up, puttem in that hole.

Did he talk to you, that Japanee man?

Japanee bin never talkin'.
No good.
Cheeky.
Puttem in handcuff now, puttem in handcuff.
He's a cunnin' bugger, yeah. Cunning bugger that, cunnin' way.
Him bin come and sneak away there.
Him bin land longa aeroplane this side where Alice Springs, this side. [We] bin go car, ridem, car, and we bin looking at him.

'Japanee, Japanee there!'

Too cheeky!
Yeah.
Takem longa jail now, lockit up, lockem up. Two-feller bin buried there, finished, die, blonga no tucker.
Too much cheeky bugger!!

Why did they die?

They never hungry, hungry. No tucker, only little bit tucker.

132 Part Two Chapter Four

Tape 3 Side 1

Good times

Tim Japangardi, Warlpiri, Yuendumu

Treated pretty well, Army time, no cheeky. Nobody get cheeky.
You know, they got provost police, and soldier policeman, somebody get cheeky. You know, they never treatem wrong way. Some people never, soldier people never, treat an Aboriginal wrong way. That's really kind.

Never. And the good fun always.

Tape 3 Side 1

Good times

Jampijinpa, Warlpiri, Willowra

Good times

The Army withdrew from all camps and settlements in March 1946, leaving its one thousand Aboriginal employees with an uncertain future. Many Aborigines realised, perhaps, that conditions could not return to pre-war.

The government, however, was concerned with problems of demobilisation. The Administrator noted with displeasure an 'acute restlessness among certain individuals', and the Native Affairs Branch concluded that a firm control should be reasserted over the Territory's Aborigines. The Yuendumu settlement, two hundred kilometres from Alice Springs, was one administrative answer to the population shifts caused by the war.

In this extract the speaker describes how he defied the order to move to the new Settlement.

When the Army ended, were you in Alice Springs, or what place?

I was in Adelaide River. We all shifted back to Alice Springs. All Bullocky Soak mob, they shift down same time. I was there two nights . . . stop there. But I just, people bin move out, I bin just come away. After that time.

[The Native Affairs Branch ordered:] 'Oh, we shift down there tomorrow, to Yuendumu, put up Yuendumu.'

The Second World War 133

It's not there *[then]*,

'Well, I'm not going that far, I'm *[going to]* walk back to Anningie *[Station]*.'

I did too.

Run away?

No, just walk up.

Did some other fellers go too?

I don't . . . know.

Just you?

Yeah. But lotta people was just get onto the truck:

'I'm not going that far. I'm going back to my home.'

A European account of life at the Alice Springs Aboriginal camp

Not recorded on accompanying tape

Johnno O'Keefe, Katherine, 9 March 1978

Anyone who wanted to, got a job. There was always a vacancy. They'd come in on their own bat, and they'd be taken to work in the morning in the trucks. They had breakfast, tea, bread and jam, that's all it consisted of . . . Then they took their lunch with them, like, they took tea, sugar and bread and stuff like that . . . But we had meat for them when they came home, and it was always either corned beef, or there would be roast or something else. And of course they always fall back on curry and rice.

There were five hundred and sixty of them there . . . They were mostly 'full-bloods'. They'd be picked up about a quarter to eight, and be back at a quarter to five. The young ones were very keen about clothes, and they weren't allowed to wear their belts. You know, the webbing belts the soldiers wore but they'd pinch them now and again, or they'd gamble them, or get them from somewhere. And it'd be all nice and bright and clean . . .

But *[the Brigadier]* cut all that stuff out. He even took the puggarees off their hats. They were good enough to **work** for the Army but that's all. He was hard on them, and to see these poor beggars digging down the drains, twelve feet *[three and a half metres]* deep, on the side of Anzac Hill, and a couple of White blokes sitting on top looking at them. All for ten pence *[eight cents]* a day. But the pay wasn't enough for what they did. They didn't get paid for what they worked for. No, no. You see that's where the class distinction came in again. There was still the same dirty work as the Whites, but they were paid as Blacks.

What sort of things did they spend their money on?

Looking glasses, lolly water and sweets of some description, and they had to have money for the pictures. You see, they had picture money there were pictures three times a week, and they had to hang on to that.

Did any of them want to go for a ceremony?

Oh, they were always having a corroboree. There was the crowd from Arltunga, the mick mob, the Catholics. Then there was the Lutheran mob, and then there was the heretics. They'd all be singing, you could sit outside on the lawn at night. Lovely lawn there, and the Hermannsburg people would start singing hymns. Oh, beautiful voices, the Hermannsburg boys had. Some were singing corroboree, singing in their own language.

Chapter Five
After the War

New legislation to govern Northern Territory Aborigines was discussed throughout 1952. The result was the 1953 Welfare Ordinance, proclaimed as a significant advance by the government, but described by a critic as 'one of the last big efforts to use authoritarian legislation to control the processes of social change'. The Administrator could declare any Aborigine to be a 'Ward' who indicated (in the opinion of Welfare officers) that he or she was in need of special care. Some 15,700 full-descent Aborigines immediately were declared to be Wards, and were now forced to continue living under a variety of restrictions including liquor consumption, the owning of property and movement.

Tape 3 Side 1

A police tracker

Tracker Tommy, Jingili, Elliott

Tracker Tommy

The relationship of Tracker Tommy, declared a Ward in 1953, was tempered by a strong personal relationship between himself and his boss, Constable Stott.

Growing up near Newcastle Waters:

Your mother and father took you to Powell Creek?

Yeah. We gettem ration, father, mother, and me, little boy. Government look afterem ration, you know, he's come here with the camel. Camel travel from Oodnadatta somewhere about, bring load to Newcastle, Powell Creek, Banka, Tennant's Creek, and Beetaloo, Newcastle.

How would you know when he was giving out rations?

Receiving rations, 1930s, Powell Creek (Photograph: J.W. Bleakley, National Library of Australia)

Native people go tellem we,

'Today ration day!'

Right, everybody come up now, come to Post Office Powell Creek, store there.

'I give you-feller ration.'

We gettem ration there, girl and boys, little boys, we get lolly too.
Get a lolly.

We go back, cookem, mother you know, longa coolamon, no more longa this, [*saucepan*] now longa coolamon. Long feller, they makem damper. They puttem longa coal. Tea boiling. Chuckem tealeaf. We little boys, they don't know about hungry. When he cook, all right, yeah, takem now.

And did that post office, they give you clothes as well?

'... cookem longa coal...'

No, only tea and sugar, tea and sugar, and jam. Government bin give it we.

What about beef, you get beef too?

No, we gettem guts. Never get a bone.
No more beef body, salt beef, corned beef. We never get it. Takem back longa camp, cookem longa coal, coverem up.

You must get hungry, though?

Well [*if*] we short, we go, hunting. Father, hunting. We

After the War 137

sit down longa shade, home place. Father killem goanna, sugarbag. We got plenty tucker home, little boy gottem, we cookembat, sort of a rubbish way.

When you were a tracker, good tucker, then, eh?

Oh, good ration, good tucker. Bread and beef, while I bin work longa job. We bin alda *[all the time]* gettem only beef, beef, bread, every day, trousers, shirt, no more money.
Tobacco. And soap, washem clothes.
Well, Bill Riley and Kennedy two-feller shift me, takem, shiftem out *[the horse]* plant, out of long' Elkedra. I bin there helpem, brandin' bullock, everything. When I bin come back, that police station. I bin work. I bin longa camp. Well Muldoon shortembat for boy *[Mounted Constable Muldoon needed a tracker]*,

'All right, we'll give you Tommy.'

'Where from?'

'Oh, from that country, from east country here.'

'Oh, I want that boy. I hearembat he good boy. Well go and tellem.'

Tracker go pickem up me. Bringem down. Say,

'Good day, good day. Where you from?'

'Newcastle my country.'

'Where you bin work?'

'Elkedra.'

'Oh, all right. You want a job?'

'Yeah. I want job.'

All right, I bin work there forty year in the police force.

Mr Muldoon, he taught you to be a tracker?

Yes, Muldoon tellem,

'You got to followem, that native people, what they bin run away in the bush.'

I followem that man, right up that camp. I know his tracks, native people.

What about dry country or rocks?

Oh, I still followem, truck followem me, behind.
Truck gottem water, you know. Police there, after me. I trackem walk. I know his track. I followem right up, findem the camp. I see-em, that's the track now. Well he's there, missing him now. See me.

'Nother one.' *[The prisoner denied the tracks were his.]*

'No, that's you track. I know you. Come on, we'll go along boss.'

Well, one time, man bin get lost, from Number Three Bore. Out this way, just out from Larrimah.
Well, two-time I bin hard work, can't findem track. I bin think about, that, what he no good longa head.
I think about all night. I bin think,

'Tommy, well, might be that man bin go out in grass.'

Well, I tellem old Stott.

[Stott had said:] 'Hey, Tommy, we gotta go back.'

'No, we got still huntem back, he's there somewhere, track I bin see-em.'

All right, we bin go longa bush, go 'long grass.
I bin losem here that track, him bin get lost. Him bin working round there, and him bin get lost.
Early morning, I look round from long way. I never get close.
Look round this way:

'Oh, that's, that's the man bin knockem grass there! That's the man bin going on longa that scrub, grass, long grass, knockem there!'

I follow him. I follow him longa short grass.

End of Tape 3 Side 1

'There, come on old fellow, he take off, this man!'

Tape 3 Side 2 Start of tape

Old Stott following me behind.
I walk.
We bin losem again — can't findem. That hard, we bin losem again. We bin come back gettem water along Number Three Bore. We bin go back, we come up and gettem more water, longa drum we bin havem.
Well, we bin going camp longside where we bin losem that track.
Well, afternoon I bin walk from morning right up to dinner. I bin come up now where he might be man bin knockem ant-bed, you know [ants nest], point. He might be knockem ant-bed.
I bin look round now:

'Oh', I bin thinking, 'there, now him bin now knockem. I see that arm where I bin missing him, that ant-bed, longa [in my] head. Yeah, know that man, bin coming bin knockem ant-bed, head. Well, you look round, yeah, where him knockem down. He's walked this way.'

We can't find him, too much stone, scrub. I bin look round now. Well, I got to go right round. I going right round, and I see-em longa hole, longa grass, big hole.

'Here that track, him bin knockem that hole, go here!'

I follow him.
All longa good ground. I bin follow him longa grass now, grass I bin see-em.

Follow him there longa grass now. We camp.
I bin followem, morning time right through. We havem dinner, we come back, start camp.
Well tomorrow, tomorrow night, might we'll go gettem water, go back. Which way Larrimah?
He [Stott] told me,

'Larrimah straight here.'

'You don't know, Tommy,'

He told me. Old Stott tellem:

'You don't know country.'

'I know my country! North!'

All right, we bin come go round gettem water longa Larrimah. We come back. Right up longa that camp. We bin followem back, tomorrow morning I bin followem, right round.
Well, him bin puttem name longa barks, longa big tree. Put his name now:

'Father, mother, no worry 'bout I'm get lost, no sorry I'm get lost, longa my head. I don't know why I'm going, to die, or alive.'

Well, I bin sing out,

'Here, that man bin markem tree here,'

I sing out longa old Stott. Come around now.

'Oh, he's put his name, put his name here, Tommy.'

'What he say?'

'Well, he say,'

' "Father, mother, no sorry I'm get lost, my brains, might findem get 'live, might I die. I no able to gettem water, never findem any water." '

There now he bin talk longa tree, talking. Him mark him, you know.
Well I still goin',

'Can you-feller find him yet?'

'We'll findem.'

I bin follow him here, that big long tree. You know, him breakem here — walk there. I follow him right through, longa grass. Well we camp like from there, we camp like that camp.
That man die. Perish.
Tomorrow morning, we havem breakfast.
Old Stott asking me — good Stott —

'Hey, Tommy, can you-feller findem today?'

'We'll findem, boss.'

'I'll take your word Tommy. We got to findem today.'

'Yes! All right!'

We bin go longa scrub again.
Well, we losem that track. We leavem here. He go this way. Well, we go wind-side. Wind come from this way, might we smellem stink. I talk, I go this way, I smell longa trees, that stink. Rot, you know? Yeah, smellem, yeah, something. Goanna bin die here.
I bin smellemabout — no.
Smellemabout — no.
He might be man there. I bin go there longa him. I bin hearem too much stink now. Find this way. I go there —
There he is! Takem out. No clothes him bin takem out. Die. No, no clothes. All right, we bin bury him.

We come right up longa Larrimah then. After finished cover him up, poor bugger. Him bin black body, you know, no more white.

He's been burned by the sun, eh?

Yes, sun bin burnt.

Was he a stockman or what?

No, he worked road party. He bin look longa head. Too much grog him bin drinking.
Too much grog.
Yes, poor bugger. I look body, oh, he's black, altogether, sun bin burnem. I takem out. I liftem, to puttem in holes, cover up with the shovel.
We bin go havem dinner longa Larrimah then.

| Tape 3 Side 2 | # You're not allowed to marry whitefeller |

Alma Gibb, Rembarrnga

Interviewed and recorded by Gill Cowlishaw.

Another restriction imposed by the Wards Ordinance was marriage. An artificial distinction was raised between 'full-bloods' (people of the full Aboriginal descent) and those generally but inaccurately known as 'half-castes' (people of part Aboriginal descent). The latter were encouraged to marry Whites, the former were intended to marry people, like themselves, of full descent.

Alma Gibb, a Rembarrnga woman of full descent, was living with a White man in the 1950s when a policeman arrived to try to force her to marry one of the three Aboriginal men he paraded in front of her.

Did they make trouble for you or for your husband most?

After the War 141

Oh, for me.

(A listener:
Both of us. She's really Aboriginal girl.)

Most for me.

They bin caught me there longa Beswick Station. We was working for contract, you know, gone up from Mainoru musterin'. They heard about, but they bin havem book *[of regulations]* you know. Somebody told them, report:

'That *[White]* man got that girl, him lay in bed,'

you see.

And, well they caughtem that man like this time, all the Welfare. Said,

'You've got one native girl there lay your bed all the time, always sleep with you.'

All the Welfare bin sleep there longa Beswick Station, and this old bloke *[the White man]* come back, and we sleep together. And he tell me story, you see.

'Eh', he said, 'talking to Welfare here. They coming afterem you.'

'Yeah?' I said. 'When?'

'They got book, everything, there. They've got to bringem up, what they've gotta do.'

'Oh yeah,' I said, 'well I see-em about *[it]* tomorrow morning,' I said. 'What you gotta, I gotta do?'

And we sleep in the stockyard.

Tomorrow morning, that Mr Morey *[policeman]* now. Carryem up, oh, big book, welfare book, you know.

(A listener:
They bin bringem that book that *[which said that]* you're not allowed to marry longa that whitefeller!)

I bin go along that Mr Morey place, longa gate they bin come up, and this, I see-em.

Oh goodness, biggest mob Welfare bin come, gottem book!

'Something wrong?'

Come up there.

'Well?' they said. 'We've got to see-em about you.'

And they callem that two boy *[men]* now. They sing out, you know, like that,

'Come on!'

This 'nother feller come up, gottem book. Signem word, you know.

What they said to you?

Oh, well they said to me,

'Well what are you going to do? Oh', he said, 'you living longa that man there.'

And old — — there then. He was with me, you know, listen to me what I want to say.

And he [*policeman*] sing out,

'I want to, we don't let you marryem this man. He's a White man. We wantem your colour!'

'Oh yeah?'

Oh, he's calling that three boys,

'Come here!'

[*Then, to Alma Gibb:*] 'What about, which one you wantem? Pick out!'

I said, I said,

'Don't let me pick that mob,' I said. 'I got nothing to do, you know. Don't want to interfere with this mob man. I don't want to marryem them. If I want to marryem, I'll marryem when I want to die and they can marry my bone!'

(A listener:
He [*she*] say, I'll stay with this old feller.)

[*The Welfare Officer:*] 'And what are you going to do now?' he said.

I said . . .

(A listener:
I'm staying with — —.)

. . . I gotta stay with this man because this man will help myself. And this man bin look after me all along you know.
No matter [*where*] we go, I'll mustering for him, you know, we mustering. Good for him, and good for me.
This man got no anybody to help [*him*]. I'll have to stay with him and I'll live with him, and I look afterem clothes for him, and bed. And we live together.

And they bin writem down.

After the War 143

Tape 3 Side 2

Two views on traditional law:
(a) You can't change the law

Nelli Camfoo Papi, Rembarrnga, Bulman

Nelli Camfoo Papi

No, we can't change it [*Aboriginal law*], we can't. Just we bin brought up and that's that our custom.

We can't go any more whitefeller ways, and forget about Aboriginal. I suppose, same as you, you can't come to bush life, you'll be sick of the bush life, and you can't change your White way, you can't come to my way. You'll be saying,

'Oh, this is not right,'

and the policeman will come up and after you.

White people think they can, I think, but then they try it for a while, they find they can't. You miss your own people, for one thing.

That's it. That the same as Aboriginal too. Say like if you and your wife take me away somewhere else, say where you want to live, might be across to London or somewhere, you want to take me there. I'll be seeing lot of White people, lot of pictures, lot of cars, lot of lights. And I can't see the sky. And I'll be saying,

Creek crossing near Bulman

144   Part Two   Chapter Five

'Well, boss, you'd better take me home to my country.'

And then when you want to say,

'No, we 'dopt you, we 'dopt you, now you are our girls for good. You can't go back to see your life again, to see your people again.'

If you say to me like that.
And I'll be cryin' and sick, and you'll put me in hospital or *[I'll]* run away, but you've still got to come up and get me. Then I'll be saying,

'You're breaking my rule and all that. I'm missing all my people.'

Tape 3 Side 2

(b) This thing should be tellem the young fellers. But nothing.

Jack Cotton Mobalily, Wambaya, Brunette Downs

Jack Cotton Mobalily

See one old feller used to say to me,

'You've gotta dance now, and you gotta have your proper mark, you know, proper culture. Or you just dance the young man *[remain uninitiated]*.'

But he wouldn't tell me. I want to know which, what is it . . .
. . . and he never even tell me. He died, and I don't still know.

Why wouldn't he tell you?

I don't know, and I still got it.

What about those young boys over there, like the kids in school here? Do they know about all the secret way or — I know they can't know it yet, they they're too young — but they — they going to be shown all that Sunday business [secret life] *different times, do you reckon?*

Couldn't tell you.

Oh, several times I was going to ask them *[to talk to the boys]* you know, tell your people anything. Like to tell those kids anything. Lot of things they can tellem.
Sacred, you know, whatsaname . . . What do you callem again? Sacred. Big sacred you can't tellem, but lot of things you **should** tellem. But they don't tellem.

They don't tellem.

See this waterhole, he got 'skin' *[mythological and kin identity]*, that water. That's *Bungarinji*.
I don't know what you callem longa your, that mob side. We callem

Bungarinji... It's *Bungarinji* country. *Bungarinji* waterhole.
He goes up there about 14 miles *[22 kilometres]*. He's two skin now, that waterhole. He goes into *Waanyi* country.

He one skin from where he start.
This country, this waterhole, bin made by two *Burrinyai [mythological figures]*. They callem two *Burrinyai* ... made that waterhole. The same as you talk about God, you know, something. I don't know.

That's right, yeah, same way.

Well this thing should be tellem the young fellers. But nothing.

What about — could you tellem?

I can't tellem.

Not in the right relation?

Mm.

What about like, old men over there. They ought to tellem?

They ought to tellem.

But they don't. Why don't they tellem?

Buggered if I know.

Because when those old men die — no one to tellem.

Nobody. Oh, no-one there.

Tape 3 Side 2

Mainoru to Bulman

Willi Martin Jaylama, Rembarrnga, Weemol

Willi Martin Jaylama

In 1965 the Commonwealth Conciliation and Arbitration Commission awarded pay to Northern Territory Aboriginal stockmen generally equal to that of Whites. The evictions of the Aboriginal communities from the stations, which began immediately and continued in some areas for two decades, occurred because the pastoral lessees maintained that they could not afford to pay the new, higher wages. The communities, as in this account, sometimes made their way to new living areas which have since become Aboriginal lands in their own right.

When the Yankee came round in the first place, well, we told him,

'This is our country.'

And they said,

'No, this is not your country.'

I told him,

'Now this our country.'

And he said,

'No, it's not your country. And we got this place to run. So if you want to go, go to the settlement *[at Beswick, some 150 kilometres away].*'

Mainoru Station

And we told him,

'We're not going to go to settlement. We're goin' bush, and stay there. And we live there, and we die there, because we belong to the country.'

We told him,

'And please give us sense. If we're going to stop up here for a couple of days, before we move, we must gonna findem water.'

It was very hot days, that day, very dry 15 mile out *[24 kilometres].* And we got small kids, carryem out, got a lot of swag, no vehicles, just walking 48 miles *[77 kilometres],* seven weeks, through the hot season. Just walk about half a mile away from the station, and stay there for 'nother couple of night, and I used to tellem, I used to tellem all the young boys,

'Just go up, if you can findem more water.'

And we used to wait for the rain, lot of rain drops, and then we'd move, because the place was really hot, we couldn't walk. Kids was walkin', and carry their own swag.
So we did that for 48 miles. Seven weeks, right up to Bulman waterhole.

When he said, go from that station, Mainoru, did he sort of get all the Aboriginal people around him, and make a speech? — or how did he tell you to go?

Oh, he said,

Saddles, Bulman

'I'm not going to feed you people, haven't got much tucker to feed you people, you'll just have to go.'

He told one of his two boss, he said,

'Righto, everybody, go on,

After the War   147

roll your swag. You know, just go. Clear off from this place, you know.'

And I said,

'Look, we're same human. Very sorry, we fight for freedom. We're going to move away every two mile [3 kilometres], we stay there. We're not animals, like you. We're all human.'

So we told him.
We spend three weeks after that, that man said, 'You go'. We spent three weeks four mile [6 kiolmetres] out from that place, Mainoru. Higher up, we stop there:

'If you come along there we're gonna all shoot a spear. That's fair!'

You know? We promise him.

Tape 3 Side 2

Elsey to Djembere (Jilkminggan)

Jess Roberts Garalnganjag, Mangarayi, Jilkminggan

Jess Roberts Garalnganjag at Jilkminggan

This account describes how the community of the old Elsey station was abandoned in Mataranka town when they left the station for the weekend. It was some time before the people were able to occupy a small excision from Elsey, now known as Jilkminngan.

We bin listen them Roper Valley mob might bin pull out from station.
Some people bin pull out from station, then, before rodeo, eh? Before the races [at] Mataranka. Pull out they bin all the way, eh?

That manager bloke and them stockmen, you know, White men, you know, stockmen, when they used to go workem up, like we were la [longa] stock camps, and they bin askem that lot, this lot boy,

'You know that Roper Valley Station — them people bin pull out from that manager. They not work.
They all that lot bin pull out. You're not going to do same thing?' him say.

'No, we can't pull out. We can't just pull out from job,' they said. 'We're going to wait till time holiday,' they bin tellem.

And even that manager bloke too, you know, that George Westmacott, he bin sorry and him bin come up talk to people like them stockboy, you know:

'You people going to pull out from me?'

'Oh, no, we won't pull out.'

Some people bin makem litttle bit of trouble, like a fight. I don't know what they bin done when they pull out from Roper Valley. I don't know what they bin doing, they might have bin fight, or argument. Or there might be stockman bin argument, or stockfight. But not us mob. He said,

'You don't, you don't pull out when you [on] your job.'

This mob bin tellem,

'We can't pull out.'

All right, we bin worried, when that show and races bin come close in the Mataranka.

Aboriginal bin saddle up: we're going now, we're going in.
Some people bin gettem taxi and some other people go in the truck, alongside the people who bin going in that taxi, in Mataranka.

That was Thursday.
From Friday, that's afternoons, and Saturday.
Sunday bin nothing.
Monday bin nothing eh. We gotta wait for lift [back to Elsey Station] now.

There's manager bloke came, you know, and ask, tell people from before that show:

'Well I'm sorry, you people, you're goin' to find your [own] way when that rodeo bin him finish.
You know, after that rodeo, you gotta, you people gotta findem your way,'

he said. Manager bloke told them people,

'Well I'm, we broke for money now, no money longa station now, no more pay you people.
And you can find your way come back where you wanna stay. Okay?'

We bin gotta wait here from Monday.
Tuesday, ten o'clock I went to store and ring up for that Welfare bloke, you know, we'll get a lift in longa people. We had plenty tucker, and I bin tellem my brother, and that Welfare to, you know, askem more people now, to bringem back us people back to Djembere [Jilkminggan] now.
And then him bin tellem in a telegram, well, we'll be here about tomorrow ten o'clock.
Wednesday.
We'll go back, tellem them people, all these people now, we goin' to wait that Welfare might come tomorrow. We'll have to wait here.

We got to wait — camp — long Wednesday, ten o'clock smoko, we saw that Welfare people come now, that Toyota, and with trailer, you know [for] swag. They came there, and him bin come askem, you know, all the people, you know, bin goin' meet him,

'What wrong?'

'[?] . . . Where we going to get lift now?'

Well Welfare bin asking,

'Well where you going to make it now?'

'Go back, go straight back to Djembere now.'

And see all day from Wednesday they bin carting people, like here.

Biggest mob.

Yeah, biggest mob. All day, sun go down.
Gotta cartem that people, all day, sun go down, and cartem next morning. Thursday cartem, cartem everything from station. Now, you know, some swag.
And people bin go gettem dog.

Tape 3 Side 2

Epilogue: following the direction
Worraki Number One and Bilu, Dharlwangu, Galiwin'ku

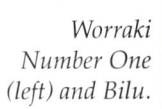

Worraki Number One (left) and Bilu.

Translated by Bilu.

Since he was young, he [*Worraki*] was working, living quiet, taking us to the hunting, show us the right way, good way. How to catch fish, how to get, got yams from the bush, honey, wild fruit.
That was his life.
He was just showing like, myself, and my families, my relations, his relations, he was showing a good thing.
And he was showing his life to our, to our new life, for us to, you know, follow that direction.
Like, my father used to do . . . his own direction, so their sons must follow their own directions, like, olden days used to. To get yams, get fish, to get maybe crab or some other wild fruit.
And that is, it's going to be happen, for ever. Like, *Yolngu*, Aborigins, is Aborigins, our songs, our sacred things, our law, and the customs, cultures, is one body.

150   Part Two   Chapter Five

And that means it's guiding *Yolngu* people in that way.

He's getting old, he's getting old now, and that means what he has done, while he was young, what was important to him, and he's thinking about that time, that olden days, younger days, that he used to be young, same like my age.
But this now, he's reckon, it's bit old for him to do that things that *[he did when]* he was young.
I'm living the way he lives, before, his direction, and that mean I have to follow his own directions.
But if I don't get that direction, otherwise, if I go to other place, or get maybe girls or someone making troubles, they'll get me.
That sort of thing.
Or even breaking the ceremonies, or other things, and he show me. That is our, our culture. But if I follow my father's direction, that mean he guide me right way, and right position.

While he was young, and up to now day, he used to teach us, how to stop, how to catch fish, turtles, crab and other things, wild yams and wild fruit. And that time, when he teach us that for every, every wild fruit from the bush.

And then he teach us how to be sensible, to be, you know, instead of making troubles, or stealing other people's wife, or killing, or hurting peoples.
And he teach us everything that he bin, his father bin teach him. And so, that was his life. And he's willing, now he's willing to teach us while we are getting older. Even the younger, youngest brother, well that's his job *[too]*, that his life. He just have to taught us into right position.
Even, even *[though]* I'm bit older, he still have to teach me, because I'm son, eldest son. Well that mean he just have to get in and teach me.

And then after that goes on to youngest to youngest. Later on, that is my chance. I have to take his place, the way he bin living here since long time from the early day up till now.
And I have to follow his directions.

End of Tape 3 Side 2